Even More QUILTS FOR BABY

Easy as A B C

URSULA REIKES

D0642325

Martingale
& COMPANY
BOTHELL, WASHINGTON

CREDITS

President . . . . Nancy J. Martin
CEO/Publisher . . . . Daniel J. Martin
Associate Publisher . . . . Jane Hamada
Editorial Director . . . . Mary V. Green
Design and Production Manager . . . . Cheryl Stevenson
Technical Editor . . . . Ursula Reikes
Copy Editor . . . . Karen Koll
Illustrator . . . . Laurel Strand
Cover and Text Design . . . . Stan Green
Photographer . . . . Brent Kane

Even More Quilts for Baby: Easy as ABC
© 2000 by Ursula Reikes

Martingale & Company
PO Box 118
Bothell, WA 98041-0118
www.patchwork.com

That Patchwork Place is an imprint of Martingale & Company.

Printed in China
04 03 02 01 00   8 7 6 5 4 3 2

Library of Congress Cataloging-in-Publication Data

Reikes, Ursula
    Even more quilts for baby : easy as ABC / Ursula Reikes.
        p. cm.
    ISBN 1-56477-282-9
    1. Quilting—Patterns. 2. Patchwork—Patterns.
    3. Crib quilts. I. Title.

TT835 .R437 2000
746.46'041—dc21   99-053398

DEDICATION

Photo by Ursula Reikes

In loving memory of my best buddy, Barney

ACKNOWLEDGMENTS

Thank you to:

My parents, Luise and Edward Golisz, for being the greatest parents in the world.

My husband, John, for helping me realize my dreams.

Trish Carey for her help in coordinating some of the fabric in the quilts. You're the greatest!

Ilona Kimmel and Sally Maxfield for their help in binding the quilts.

Betsy, Jeanne, and John Kolb for their help in holding the quilts as I worked on the designs—over and over and over again. Also to Betsy and Jeanne for helping me think of names for all 40 quilts.

And thank you to Kelsul, Inc., for providing Quilters Dream Cotton, 100% cotton batting. It is truly a dream to quilt on.

MISSION STATEMENT

We are dedicated to providing quality products and service by working together to inspire creativity and to enrich the lives we touch.

TABLE OF CONTENTS

INTRODUCTION

I never imagined that I would be writing a third book on baby quilts. However, the response to my first two books, *Quilts for Baby: Easy as ABC*, and *More Quilts for Baby: Easy as ABC*, has been so overwhelming, and the requests for another book so great, that I was inspired to do another one. Like the first two, this book contains baby quilts that are quick and easy to make. What makes this book extra special is that each of the twenty quilt designs is shown in two versions: one in bright fabrics and one in pastel fabrics. Having two versions of every quilt gives you the opportunity to see a quilt design in two extremes so that you can choose the one that appeals to you.

The number of fabrics required to make the baby quilts varies from two to five. If you're in a hurry, choose a simple one like the H Block (page 18), which requires only two fabrics. Kathy Ezell, a good friend, discovered that it took only one hour to make the H Block pattern. With another two hours to machine quilt it and bind it, she had made a quilt in three hours.

All the quilts are small, which makes them quick to assemble. There are also nine quilts without borders, making the process even faster. You can easily make any one of the nine quilts tonight and take it to a baby shower tomorrow. If you need a larger quilt, remember that you can enlarge any of them simply by making more blocks or adding more borders.

Most of the blocks are traditional and have been used by quilters for years, but I have altered some of the blocks to make them easier to make. If you are new to quilting, start with one of the first ten quilts, which are the easiest. If you are a seasoned quilter, you'll enjoy making any of the quilts. I think everyone will be pleasantly surprised at just how quickly and easily these baby quilts come together.

Many quilt groups and guilds across the country have used the patterns in my previous books to make baby quilts for charitable organizations and hospitals. Here is another collection of simple patterns that you can use to make wonderful quilts for some very deserving children.

Whether you're making baby quilts to give to friends or to donate, have fun creating these quick and easy quilts.

GENERAL DIRECTIONS

ANATOMY OF A QUILT

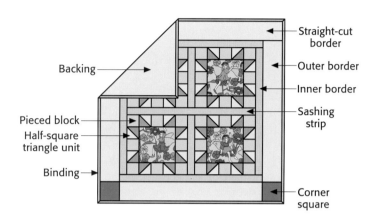

Backing: A large piece of fabric that covers the back of a quilt. For larger quilts, it may be constructed from more than one piece of fabric.

Batting: A layer inside the quilt, sandwiched between the quilt top and the quilt backing.

Binding: A strip of fabric, cut on either the straight of grain or the bias, sewn to and wrapped around the edges of the quilt to finish it.

Borders: The area surrounding the main body of the quilt top that acts like a frame on a picture. One or more fabric strips of varying widths may be added. *Borders with straight-cut corners* are applied in two steps: border strips are sewn to opposite side edges of the quilt top first, then to the top and bottom edges. *Borders with corner squares* are applied in three steps: border strips are sewn to opposite side edges of the quilt top first, then corner squares are sewn to each end of the remaining border strips. Finally, the border strips with corner squares attached are sewn to the top and bottom edges.

Corner Square: A square of fabric used to join adjacent border strips.

Half-Square Triangle Unit: A square made up of two right-angle triangles.

Pieced Block: Small pieces of fabric in various shapes sewn together to form a larger design.

Quilt Top: The upper quilt layer, which forms the overall design.

Sashing Strips: A strip of fabric sewn between the blocks and between rows of blocks.

SUPPLIES

You will need a few basic supplies to make the quilts in this book:
- 100% cotton fabric
- 100% good quality cotton thread for stitching
- Lightweight 100% cotton or cotton/polyester batting
- Cotton, rayon, or transparent monofilament thread for machine quilting
- Sewing machine in good working order, with a walking foot or darning foot for machine quilting
- Fine, thin pins
- Fabric scissors
- Seam ripper
- Marking pencil
- Safety pins or QuilTak basting gun

Rotary-cutting equipment, including the following items:
- rotary cutter
- cutting mat
- 6" x 24" ruler
- 12" x 12" ruler for squaring up blocks; 15" x 15" is helpful for larger blocks
- 6" x 6" Omnigrid ruler for cutting the blocks on page 56
- 6½" x 6½" Omnigrid for cutting the blocks on page 70

SELECTING FABRICS

Finding that special fabric for that special baby is the fun part of making a quilt. I'm always on the lookout for colorful, whimsical prints that I know will make babies smile—prints that will catch their eyes and make them explore the surface of the quilts as they feel the softness. Since infants see bright colors before they see pastels, I prefer to make baby quilts that are bright and bold. My motto is "the brighter, the better." But many people making baby quilts do not share my view. And that's okay. As you can see by looking at the quilts in this book, the quilts are just as much fun in pastel colors as they are in brighter colors.

I prefer 100% cotton fabric because it is easy to work with and launders beautifully. Baby quilts are washed so frequently that it's worth the extra money to buy good quality cottons that can withstand the agitation of a washer and the heat of a dryer.

When selecting fabrics for baby quilts, consider the following:
- Combine pure colors (primary colors) with other pure colors.
- Combine tints (pastels) with other tints.
- Vary the scale of the busyness of the prints.
- Try tone-on-tone solids in addition to plain solids. I love the Moda Marbles fabric by Moda Fabrics. They come in an assortment of colors and have a subtle tone-on-tone texture that adds a little life to a quilt.

Don't be afraid to mix dots, plaids, and stripes all in one quilt—in primary color quilts as well as pastel quilts. It is the mix of different prints that adds interest to a quilt. Remember, babies are just starting to explore their worlds, and the more stimuli they have, the better.

Many of the quilts contain a large square in which to feature a fun fabric. Cutting motifs from large-scale prints can present some problems. If the motifs are close together, you can cut strips across the fabric width and then crosscut the strip into squares. If the motifs are farther apart and you don't want as much of the background in your squares, you will need to "fussy cut" the motifs. I had to do this to cut 8½" squares from the fabric in "Busy Bears" (page 40).

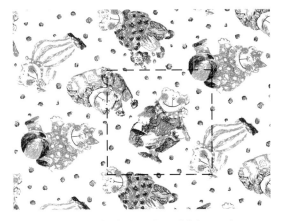

Cutting specific designs from fabric requires extra yardage. Plan your cuts carefully.

Fussy cutting is easy to do with a square ruler. To help you see the desired size square, place a piece of masking tape on the ruler along the appropriate markings; for example, on the 8½" mark for 8½" squares. Do this in both directions.

Masking tape

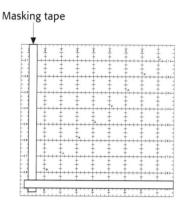

Move the marked square ruler around the fabric to isolate a motif. Cut the first two sides of the square. Next, turn the ruler around and align the desired markings with the just-cut edges and cut the remaining two sides.

You can also cut a piece of template plastic in the desired size. Move the template around the fabric to isolate a motif. Draw around the plastic template with a pencil and cut the square out with scissors. I don't recommend cutting around template plastic with a rotary cutter. If you cut into the plastic, you may ruin the template.

PREPARING FABRICS

Fabrics don't get into my sewing room unless they are prewashed. This way I don't have to stop and think about whether a piece of fabric on my shelf has been washed or not. I prewash fabrics in warm water, without detergent, then tumble dry and iron them.

YARDAGE REQUIREMENTS

The yardage requirements for the quilts in this book are based on at least 42" of usable width **after prewashing**. If your fabric is narrower than 42" wide, you may need to cut additional strips from additional yardage to get the required pieces. It's a good idea to double-check the fabric width at the quilt store.

In most of my quilts, you'll see that the theme fabric is often used in the borders. However, these two items are listed separately in the Materials and Cutting charts in case you want to use two different fabrics. If you want to use the same fabric, add the yardage amounts together.

ROTARY CUTTING

Directions are for rotary cutting all pieces, and all measurements include ¼"-wide seam allowances. The blade on a rotary cutter is very sharp. Keep it away from children and remember to engage the safety guard after every cut.

1. Fold the fabric, wrong sides together, matching the selvages and aligning the crosswise and lengthwise grains as much as possible. Place the folded edge closest to you on the cutting mat.
2. Align a square ruler along the folded edge of the fabric. Place a long, straight ruler to the left of the square, just covering the uneven raw edges of the fabric. Remove the square ruler and cut along the right-hand edge of the ruler, rolling the rotary cutter away from you. Discard this strip. (Reverse this procedure if you are left-handed.)

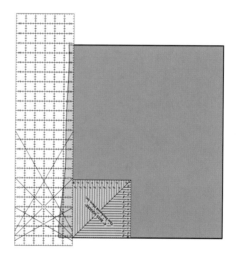

3. To cut strips, align the required measurement on the ruler with the newly cut edge of the fabric. For example, to cut a 2½" wide strip, place the 2½" mark of the ruler on the edge of the fabric.

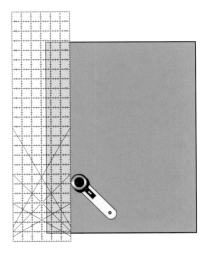

4. To cut squares and rectangles, cut strips in the required widths. Remove the selvage ends of the strip. Align the required measurements on the ruler with the left edge of the strip and cut a square or rectangle. Continue cutting until you have the required number of pieces.

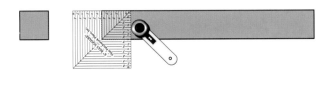

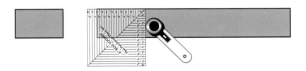

5. For some quilts, you will cut strips, sew them together in strip sets, and then cut segments from the strip sets. First, trim the ends of the strip set to square it up. Second, align the required measurement on the ruler with the left edge of the strip set and cut the specified number of segments.

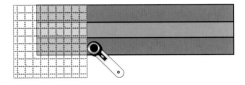

CUTTING TRIANGLES

Two different triangles are used to make some of the quilts in this book. The difference between them is the direction of the straight grain. The lengthwise grain runs parallel to the selvages, and the crosswise grain runs across the width of the fabric. Both are considered the straight grain.

On half-square triangles the straight grain is on the short sides, and on quarter-square triangles it is on the long side.

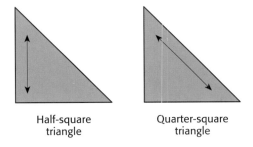

Half-square triangle   Quarter-square triangle

For half-square triangles, cut a square the size indicated in the cutting chart. Cut the square once diagonally. This symbol ◻ is used to indicate when to cut half-square triangles.

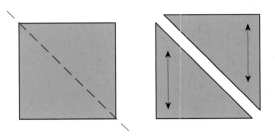

For quarter-square triangles, cut a square the size indicated in the cutting chart. Cut the square twice diagonally. This symbol ⊠ is used to indicate when to cut quarter-square triangles.

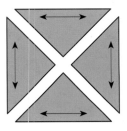

PIECING

The single most important thing to remember is to maintain a consistent ¼"-wide seam allowance throughout your piecing. Otherwise, your block will not be the desired finished size. If that happens, the size of everything else in the quilt is affected—alternate blocks, sashing, and borders. Measurements for all components of the quilt are based on blocks that finish to the desired size plus ¼" all around for seams.

CREATING AN ACCURATE SEAM GUIDE

Take the time to establish an exact ¼"-wide seam guide on your machine. Some sewing machines have a special quilting foot. With these, you can use the edge of the presser foot to guide the edge of the fabric for a perfect ¼"-wide seam.

If you don't have such a foot, create a seam guide with masking tape so it will be easy to stitch a ¼"-wide seam.

1. Place a ruler or piece of graph paper with 4 squares to the inch under your presser foot.
2. Gently lower the needle onto the first ¼" line from the right-hand edge of the ruler or paper. Place several layers of masking tape or a piece of moleskin (available in drugstores) along the right-hand edge of the ruler or paper, in front of the needle. Test your new guide to make sure your seams are ¼" wide; if they are not, readjust your seam guide.

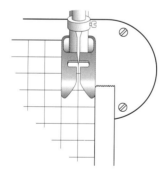

PIECING HALF-SQUARE TRIANGLE UNITS

Three of the patterns in this book—Sickle (page 46), Four-X Star (page 60), and Double Attic Windows (page 72) —require half-square triangle units. Use the following method to make these units.

1. Cut squares the size given in the quilt directions. Draw a diagonal line from corner to corner on the wrong side of the lightest fabric. This is your cutting line. Draw another set of lines ¼" away from the drawn line. These are your sewing lines.

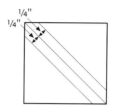

2. Place the square with the drawn line on top of a square of the contrasting fabric, right sides together. Stitch on the drawn sewing lines, or ¼" away from the center line on both sides.

3. Cut on the drawn center line. Open the unit and press the seams toward the darker fabric. Each pair of squares yields 2 half-square triangle units.

BASTING INTERSECTIONS

I learned a great tip from world-famous author and quilter Carol Doak about basting key matching points when joining pieces in blocks and when assembling rows of blocks. I used to spend quite a bit of time undoing and redoing matching points on blocks to get them perfect. Now, with Carol's basting tip, I get the points perfect every time.

Pin the beginning and end of the pieces and the seam intersections as you would normally. Set the stitch length on your machine to a basting stitch (five or six stitches per inch on most machines). Take a few stitches at the beginning of the pieces. Lift the presser foot, move the pieces to the seam intersection, and baste across the intersection. Lift the presser foot again and move to the next intersection, if there is one, or to the end of the pieces.

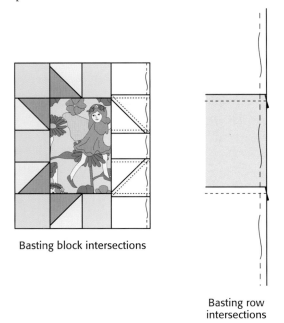

Basting block intersections

Basting row
intersections

Remove the pieces from the machine, remove the pins, and open the pieces. Are the intersections perfect? If they are, reset the machine to the standard stitch length, ten or twelve stitches per inch, and sew the pieces together from beginning to end, stitching over the basting stitches. If the points do not match, pull the bobbin thread, then the top thread, and baste again.

While it may sound like this takes a lot of extra time, think about how much time you'll save by not unsewing and resewing.

PINNING

Please take the time to pin pieces together when assembling the blocks and the quilt top. On most machines, there is a tendency for the pieces to shift slightly as they are fed under the presser foot. A few carefully placed pins will keep this shifting to a minimum. Don't risk the possibility of unaligned seams or mismatched corners and points just to a save a few minutes. Pin!

PRESSING

I use a steam iron on a cotton setting to press all seams. Since all my fabrics are prewashed and ironed, I don't worry about pieces shrinking from the heat or steam of the iron. Press each seam after stitching and before adding other pieces.

1. Press the stitches flat along a seam line before pressing the seams to one side. This relaxes the thread and smooths out any puckers.

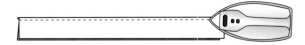

2. Working from the right side, press the seam toward the darker fabric. Use the edge of the iron to push the fabric over the seam. Be careful not to stretch the pieces out of shape as you press.

Pressing arrows ⟶ are provided in many illustrations, where the direction in which you press the seams is important. Following these arrows will help in constructing the blocks and assembling the quilt top.

SQUARING UP THE BLOCKS

No matter how carefully you sew, some blocks may end up a little smaller or a little larger than the required size. Trying to sew different-sized blocks together is very frustrating. You can do a certain amount of easing, but the results are less than satisfactory. Don't try to join blocks of different sizes; it's easier to spend time trimming blocks to one size.

Measure all the blocks for the quilt. If they are within 1/16" of each other, you shouldn't have a problem sewing them together. But, if they differ in size by 1/8" or more, square them up.

Determine which block is the smallest and trim all the other blocks to match. For example, if your blocks should be 10½" before you sew them together, and you wind up with several that are 10⅜" or 10¼", you'll need to trim all of them to 10¼". Reducing the size of the blocks by this small amount doesn't really matter. You will, however, have to reduce the size of other components, such as sashing strips and borders. For example, if the quilt you're making has sashing strips between the blocks, cut the sashing strips to match the blocks—in this case 10¼" long.

Use a rotary cutter and square ruler to trim the blocks. If, as in the example above, you are trimming to 10¼", place a piece of masking tape on the 10¼" horizontal and vertical lines of a square ruler. This makes it easy to identify the required size on the ruler. Next, find the center of the 10¼" area, which is 5⅛". Mark this spot with a pencil or a small piece of masking tape.

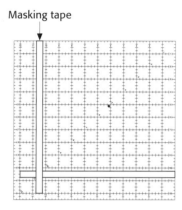

Masking tape

The most important thing to remember now is to cut from all four sides; otherwise, your blocks will be lopsided. Place the ruler on a block so that the 5⅛" center is on the center of the block. Trim along the first two sides of the block.

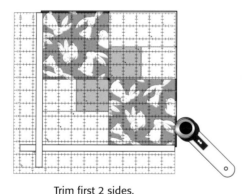

Trim first 2 sides.

Turn the block around, aligning the 10¼" marks with the newly cut edges of the block, and trim the remaining two sides.

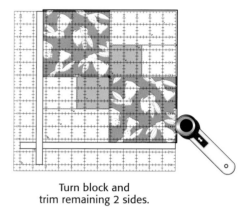

Turn block and
trim remaining 2 sides.

I know this sounds like it takes a lot of time, but you'll be glad you did it when you start sewing your blocks together.

ASSEMBLING THE QUILT TOP

When you have made all the blocks and cut all the remaining pieces, it's time to put them together to make the quilt top.

1. Arrange the blocks following the illustration provided with each quilt. Rotate the blocks as needed so that final seams of the blocks will butt together. Pressing arrows are provided to show you the direction of the seams.

2. Join the blocks in horizontal rows. Press the seams in opposite directions from row to row so opposing seams will butt against each other when you join the rows. Some quilts have specific directions for pressing the seams between blocks.

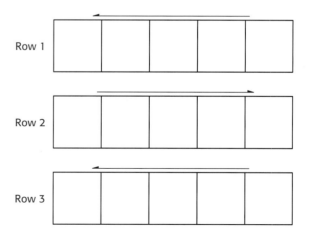

Row 1

Row 2

Row 3

3. Join the rows, making sure to match the seams between the blocks.

For quilts with sashing strips, follow the illustration to arrange the blocks and sashing strips. Join the blocks and vertical sashing strips in rows; press the seams toward the sashing strips. Join the rows of blocks and horizontal sashing strips.

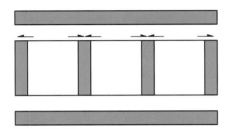

FINISHING THE QUILT

ADDING BORDERS

For the simple quilts in this book, I prefer borders with straight-cut-corners, and I generally repeat the main fabric in the border. This makes the decision about what fabric to use in the border an easy one.

In a busy non-directional print, the most fabric-efficient way to cut borders is on the crosswise grain (across the width of the fabric). If you are working with a directional print, you can position the borders so the designs all face toward the center or away from the center of the quilt. If you prefer to have the design in a directional print face the same direction in all the borders, you will need to cut two borders from the crosswise grain, and two borders from the lengthwise grain. You will need to purchase extra fabric to do this. The borders in "Pixies and Posies" (page 60) were cut so that the pixies all face the same direction.

It's important to measure and cut border strips to fit your quilt. Cutting strips and sewing them directly to the quilt top without measuring often results in a quilt with wavy borders. The edges of a quilt may be slightly longer than the distance through the center due to stretching during construction. Sometimes, each edge is a different length.

Specific measurements are provided for cutting the border strips for each quilt. These measurements are based on blocks sewn with accurate ¼"-wide seam allowances. Measure your blocks to be sure they are the correct size. To be safe, measure your quilt top after the blocks are sewn together to determine the correct border lengths.

BORDERS WITH STRAIGHT-CUT CORNERS

1. Measure the length of the quilt top through the center. Cut 2 border strips to that measurement. Mark the center of the quilt edges and the border strips.

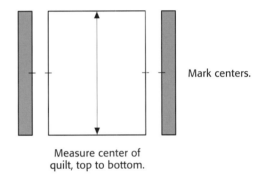

Mark centers.

Measure center of quilt, top to bottom.

2. Pin the borders to the sides of the quilt top, matching the center marks and ends and easing as necessary. Sew the borders in place. Press the seams toward the border.
3. Measure the width of the quilt top through the center, including the side borders just added. Cut border strips to that measurement. Mark, pin, and sew the borders in place as described for the side borders. Press the seams toward the border.

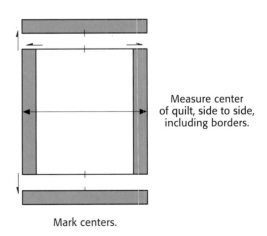

Measure center of quilt, side to side, including borders.

Mark centers.

BORDERS WITH CORNER SQUARES

Five of the patterns in this book have corner squares. This is an economical use of fabric since you can use shorter border strips. It's also a place to add another spot of color. If you prefer not to use corner squares, measure and cut border strips following directions for borders with straight-cut corners. You may need extra fabric to do this, so check your measurements.

1. Measure the width and length of the quilt top through the center. Cut border strips to those measurements. Mark the center of the quilt edges and the border strips. Pin the side borders to opposite side edges of the quilt, matching the centers and ends and easing as necessary. Sew them in place. Press the seams toward the borders.

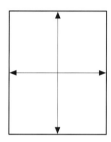

2. Sew a corner square to each end of the remaining border strips. Press the seams toward the border strip. Pin the borders to the top and bottom edges, matching the centers, seams, and ends and easing as necessary. Sew them in place. Press the seams toward the border.

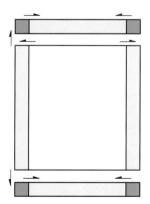

BACKING

There's no reason the backing can't be as much fun as the front of the quilt. I often use the same theme print for the backing that was used on the front. In case I don't have enough of the theme print, I'll find something that complements the fabrics on the front. Polka dots are among my favorite prints to use for backings. I always keep several yards in different colors on hand.

Cut the backing 2"–3" longer and 2"–3" wider than the quilt top. This allows for any shifting of the layers that may occur while quilting and for the slight shrinkage that occurs when the layers are quilted. Most of the quilts in this book are small enough that 42"-wide fabric will be large enough to use for the backing.

ADDING A STRIP TO THE BACKING

There are, however, two patterns that are too large for 42"-wide fabric (Nine Patch [page 30] and Double Attic Window [page 72]). If your fabric happens to be 44" wide, it may be wide enough to use as a backing. The easiest way to make a larger backing is to add a narrow strip of fabric to the length of the backing. Cut additional strips of fabric 3" to 4" wide and sew them to the 42"-wide fabric. Depending on the length of the quilt, you may need to sew two strips together before joining this extra piece to the backing. Yardage requirements for the backings on these two patterns include extra fabric so that you can do this.

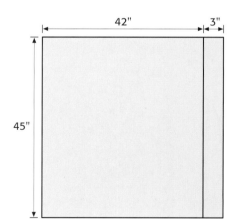

PIECING THE BACKING FROM LEFTOVERS

I often piece the backing from leftover fabrics instead of buying more fabric. To do this, determine the required backing size and cut leftover fabrics into strips or squares. Sew them together randomly or in an interesting pattern until you achieve the required size. For one of the backings, I used three large pieces of fabric left over from the front. When I sewed them together, they were still a little too narrow for the quilt, so I added another strip to one side to make the backing large enough.

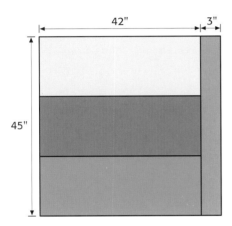

MAKING THE QUILT SANDWICH

The quilt sandwich is made up of the quilt top, batting, and backing. A thin, low-loft batting works well for either hand or machine quilting. My favorite batting is Quilters Dream Cotton—Select, from Kelsul, Inc. It is 100% pure cotton batting and it is truly a dream to quilt on. It holds the layers of the quilt together so well that I don't need to baste very much. You can stitch up to 8" apart, which allows for a lot of flexibility in your quilting designs.

1. Unroll the batting and let it relax overnight before you layer your quilt. Cut the backing and batting 2"–3" longer and 2"–3" wider than the quilt top.
2. Place the backing, wrong side up, on a large table. Use masking tape to anchor the backing to the table. Make sure the backing is flat and wrinkle-free, but be careful not to stretch it out of shape.

3. Place the batting on top of the backing, smoothing out all wrinkles.
4. Center the pressed quilt top, right side up, on top of the batting. Smooth out any wrinkles. Make sure the quilt-top edges are parallel to the backing edges.
5. Baste with safety pins or a QuilTak basting gun (available in most quilt shops). Place pins 6"–8" apart, away from the area you intend to quilt. Sewing machines and safety pins do not get along!

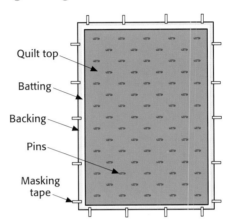

QUILTING

All of my quilts are machine quilted because I don't have the time to hand quilt. If you have the time, by all means hand quilt. But if you're like me and want to make sure the babies get the quilts before they learn to drive, you'll want to take the easy way out and either machine quilt them yourself or have them machine quilted by a professional. The thought of machine quilting all forty of the quilts in this book was overwhelming, so I enlisted the aid of a professional machine quilter to do seventeen of them.

Most of the quilts are quilted with a combination of straight-line and free-motion quilting. I use either cotton or rayon thread for machine quilting, depending on the color I need. Finding a thread color to blend with all the prints can be difficult, but red seems to work with most of the primary-colored quilts. White or off-white seems to work well for the pastel-colored quilts. Variegated threads also work well for multicolored quilt tops.

TIP: I USE A TOPSTITCH (130 N) NEEDLE, SIZE 80/12, FOR MACHINE QUILTING. IT HAS A LARGE NEEDLE EYE THAT PREVENTS THE THREAD FROM FRAYING AND BREAKING.

STRAIGHT-LINE QUILTING

You will need a walking foot to help feed the quilt layers through the machine without causing them to shift or pucker. I also use a walking foot when using decorative stitches. The Pfaff sewing machine has a built-in walking foot that I love. Other machines require a separate attachment.

Walking foot

Use straight-line quilting to stitch straight lines, to outline quilt, and to quilt in the ditch.

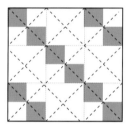

Diagonal straight lines

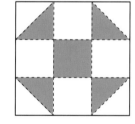

Outline quilt   Quilt in the ditch

FREE-MOTION QUILTING

You will need a darning foot and the ability to drop or cover the feed dogs on your sewing machine. With free-motion quilting, you do not turn the fabric under the needle, but instead guide the fabric in the direction of

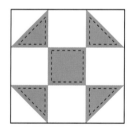

Darning foot

the design. This technique requires some practice. I recommend that you practice for several hours before starting on a quilt.

Use free-motion quilting to stipple quilt, outline-quilt a motif in the fabric, or create loops, hearts, and many other designs.

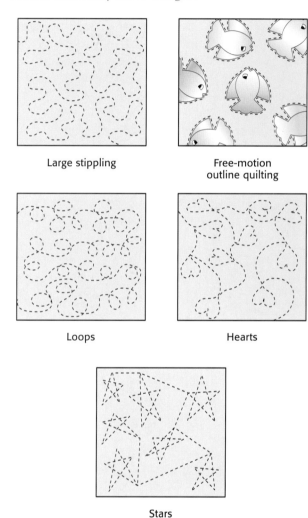

Large stippling

Free-motion outline quilting

Loops

Hearts

Stars

TIP: SEE MAURINE NOBLE'S BOOK, MACHINE QUILTING MADE EASY, FOR SOME QUICK AND SIMPLE METHODS OF TYING OR TACKING A QUILT BY MACHINE, PLUS MANY OTHER MACHINE-QUILTING TIPS.

BINDING

I prefer a double-fold, straight-grain binding. I use a double-fold, bias binding only when I want to change the direction of a print for the binding, such as when I place a stripe on the diagonal. See "Buttercup Blues" (page 44), "Blast Off!" (page 62), and "Giggling Gators" (page 76) for examples.

To cut double-fold, straight-grain binding strips follow these guidelines:

Cut the required number of 2¼"-wide strips across the width of the fabric. You will need enough 2¼"-wide strips to go around the perimeter of the quilt plus 10" for seams and the mitered fold in the corners.

Follow these steps to cut double-fold, bias binding strips:

1. Fold the fabric for the binding as shown. Pay careful attention to the location of the lettered corners.

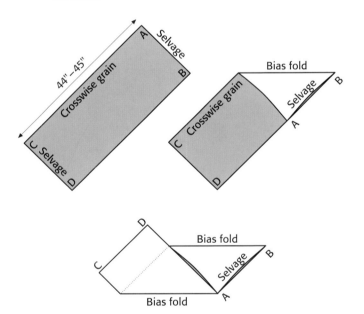

2. Cut strips 2¼" wide, cutting perpendicular to the folds as shown.

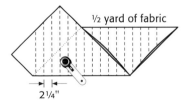

½ yard of fabric

2¼"

Follow these steps to attach the binding:

1. Trim the batting and backing even with the edges of the quilt top.
2. Join binding strips, right sides together, to make 1 long piece of binding. Press the seams open.

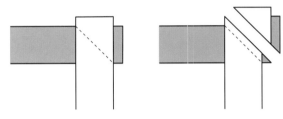

Joining straight-cut strips

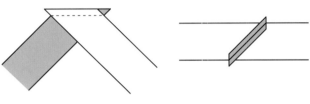

Joining bias-cut strips

3. Fold the binding in half, wrong sides together; press.
4. Leaving the first 10" of binding unsewn, stitch the binding in place, using a ¼"-wide seam allowance. Stop stitching ¼" from the corner of the quilt and backstitch. Clip the thread.

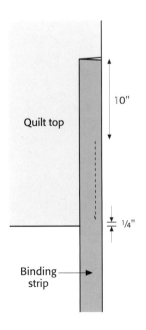

10"

Quilt top

¼"

Binding strip

5. Turn the quilt so you will be stitching down the next side. Fold the binding up, away from the quilt. Next, fold the binding back down onto itself, keeping the fold parallel with the edge of the quilt top. Begin stitching at the edge, backstitching to secure.

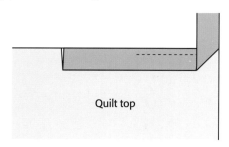

Quilt top

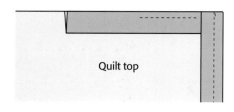

Quilt top

6. Repeat steps 4 and 5 on the remaining edges and corners of the quilt. When you are within 10" of the starting point, remove the quilt from the sewing machine and lay the unsewn section on a flat surface. Fold the unsewn binding ends back on themselves so they just meet in the middle over the unsewn area of the quilt top. Finger-press or pin both bindings to mark this junction.

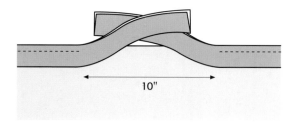

10"

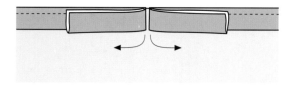

7. Unfold both sides of the bindings and match the centers of the pressed Xs. Sew across the

intersection as when sewing the binding strips together. Trim the excess fabric and press the seam open. Finish stitching the binding to the quilt edge.

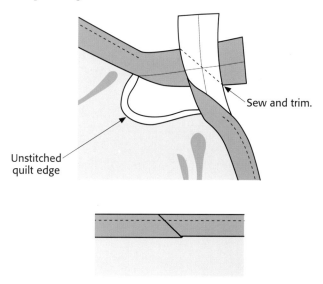

Sew and trim.

Unstitched quilt edge

8. Fold the binding over the raw edges to the back. Blindstitch in place, with the folded edge covering the row of machine stitching. A miter will form at each corner. Blindstitch the mitered corners in place.

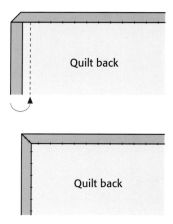

Quilt back

Quilt back

ADDING A LABEL

Don't forget to make a label for your quilt. Include your name, city, and state, the date, and the recipient if it is a gift. You can write the information on a piece of muslin with a permanent marking pen or machine embroider it. Sew the label to the back of the finished quilt.

THE QUILTS

Now that you understand the basic techniques, it's time to choose a pattern, buy some fun fabrics, and make a quilt. In the following pages, you'll find directions for twenty patterns, along with two examples of each pattern—one in pastels and one in brighter colors.

All of the quilts are easy to make. I have arranged them, however, based on the length of time it takes to make them. Some of the quilts can be made in only two or three hours, while others can be made in an afternoon or an evening. The first ten should come together most quickly. So review the quick reminders before getting started, and remember to have fun.

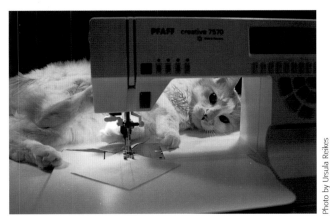

This was Barney's favorite spot while I worked on the quilts for this book.

QUICK REMINDERS:
- Prewash all your fabrics.
- Measure twice, cut once.
- ◹ = cut squares once diagonally (page 7).
- ⧅ = cut squares twice diagonally (page 7).
- Be sure your seam allowances are ¼" wide.
- Pin seam intersections before stitching.
- Press the seams after each step.
- Pay attention to the pressing arrows.

EXTRA TIPS FOR AN E.E.E.
(Especially Enjoyable Experience)
- Put on a pot of tea or coffee, or make sure your favorite beverage is at the ready.
- Make sure plenty of chocolate is on hand (for me, M&Ms always hit the spot—they melt in your mouth, not on your fabric!).
- Start up some energetic music or your favorite old movie, or enjoy a few hours of talk radio.
- Invite your cat or dog to join in the fun (if they don't invite themselves!).
- Relax, snuggle into your most comfortable chair, and start stitching!

H BLOCK

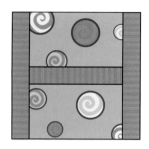

H Block
Finished size: 11"

MATERIALS			CUTTING	
42"-wide fabric			Cut all strips across the fabric width	
Fabric	**Yardage**		**# of Strips**	**Strip Size**
Theme print	⅞ yd.		4	5¼" x 42"
			2	5¼" x 10"
Fabric A	⅝ yd.		8	2" x 42"
			1	2" x 10"
Backing	1 yd.			
Binding	⅜ yd.		4	2¼" x 42"
Batting	37" x 37"			

Sweet Swirls
by Ursula Reikes,
1999, Ivins, Utah,
33½" x 33½"
Machine quilted
by Janice Nelson.

Alternate quilt
Road Rally
(see page 26)

DIRECTIONS

1. Make 3 strip sets in 2 different lengths. Cut 9 segments, each 8½" wide.

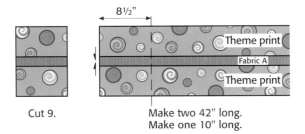

Cut 9.　　　　Make two 42" long.
　　　　　　　Make one 10" long.

2. Place 3 segments next to each other on top of a 2" x 42" Fabric A strip, right sides together. Do not overlap the edges of the segments. Stitch. Do not cut apart yet.

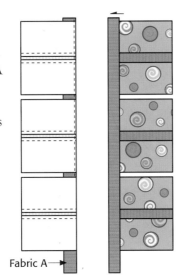

Fabric A →

3. Turn the strip of sewn segments upside down and place the opposite side of the segments on top of another 2" x 42" Fabric A strip, right sides together. Stitch.

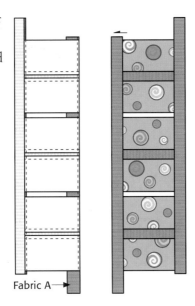

Fabric A →

4. Lay the sewn unit on the cutting mat. Use a ruler and rotary cutter to cut between the segments, trimming away any excess fabric. Repeat steps 2–4 with the remaining segments and Fabric A strips.

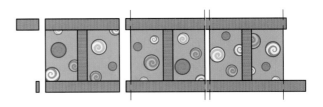

5. Arrange the blocks in 3 rows of 3 blocks each.

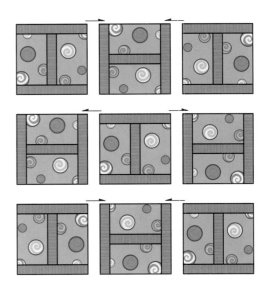

6. Join the blocks in horizontal rows. Join the rows.
7. Layer the quilt top with batting and backing; baste. Quilt as desired.
8. Bind the edges and add a label.

BASKET WEAVE

Unit 1
Finished size: 6"

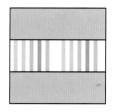

Unit 2
Finished size: 6"

CUTTING
Cut all strips across the fabric width

Fabric	Yardage	# of Strips	Strip Size
Theme print	½ yd.	6	2½" x 42"
Fabric A	½ yd.	6	2½" x 42"
Fabric B	½ yd.	6	2½" x 42"
Backing	1⅛ yds.		
Binding	⅜ yd.	4	2¼" x 42"
Batting	39" x 39"		

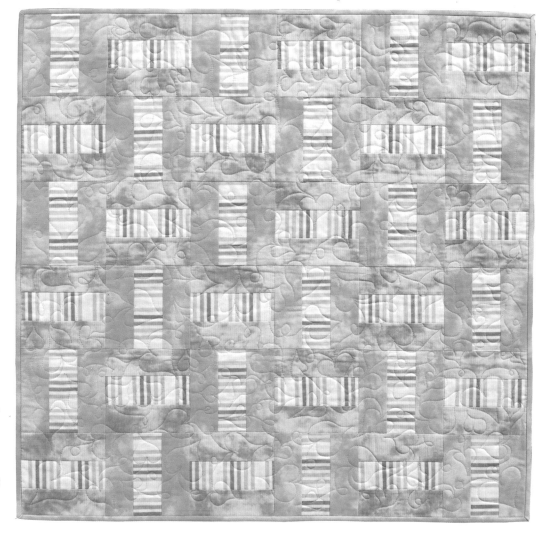

Rainbow Weave
by Ursula Reikes,
1999, Ivins, Utah,
36½" x 36½"

Alternate quilt
Bright Beginnings
(see page 27)

DIRECTIONS

1. Make 3 each of Strip Sets #1 and #2. Cut 6 units, each 6½" wide, from each strip set.

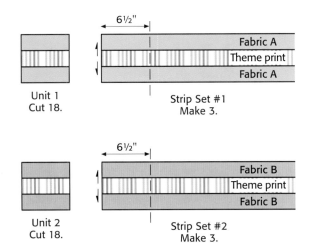

Unit 1
Cut 18.

6½"

Fabric A
Theme print
Fabric A

Strip Set #1
Make 3.

6½"

Fabric B
Theme print
Fabric B

Unit 2
Cut 18.

Strip Set #2
Make 3.

2. Arrange the units in 6 rows of 6 units each.

3. Join the blocks in horizontal rows. Join the rows.
4. Layer the quilt top with batting and backing; baste. Quilt as desired.
5. Bind the edges and add a label.

SIMPLE PATCH

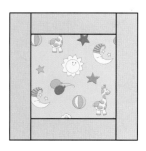

Simple Patch
Finished size: 9"

MATERIALS		CUTTING			
42"-wide fabric		Cut all strips across the fabric width			
		FIRST CUT		**SECOND CUT**	
Fabric	**Yardage**	**# of Strips**	**Strip Size**	**# of Pieces**	**Piece Size**
Theme print	¼ yd.	1	6½" x 42"		
Fabric A	½ yd.	5	2" x 42"		
		1	3½" x 42"	12	3½" x 3½"
Fabric B	⅝ yd.	5	3½" x 42"	17	3½" x 9½"
Backing	1¼ yds.				
Binding	⅜ yd.	4	2¼" x 42"		
Batting	30" x 42"				

setting
sashing

Baby Dreams by
Ursula Reikes, 1999,
Ivins, Utah,
27½" x 39½".

Alternate quilt
Wacky Wabbits
(see page 28)

DIRECTIONS

1. Make 1 strip set. Cut 6 segments, each 6½" wide.

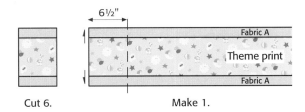

Cut 6.   Make 1.

2. Place 4 segments next to each other on top of a 2" x 42" Fabric A strip, right sides together. Do not overlap the edges of the segments. Stitch. Do not cut apart yet.

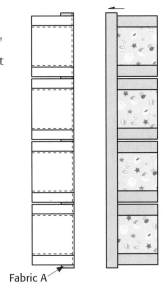

Fabric A

3. Turn the strip of sewn segments upside down and place the opposite side of the segments on top of another 2" x 42" Fabric A strip, right sides together. Stitch.

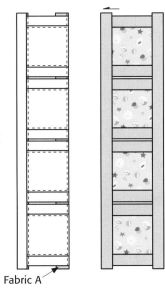

Fabric A

4. Lay the sewn unit on the cutting mat. Use a ruler and rotary cutter to cut between the segments, trimming away any excess fabric. Repeat steps 2–4 with the remaining 2 segments and Fabric A strip (cut the strip in half).

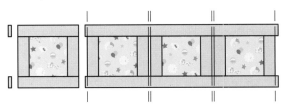

5. Arrange the blocks, squares, and rectangles in rows.

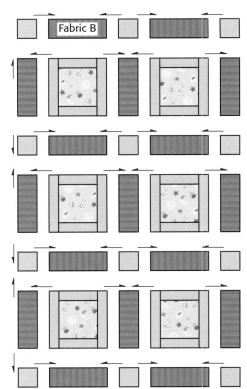

6. Join the units in horizontal rows. Join the rows.
7. Layer the quilt top with batting and backing; baste. Quilt as desired.
8. Bind the edges and add a label.

BARNEY'S BLOCK

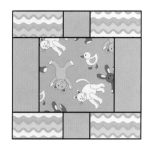

Barney's Block
Finished size: 12"

MATERIALS		CUTTING	
42"-wide fabric		Cut all strips across the fabric width	
Fabric	**Yardage**	**# of Strips**	**Strip Size**
Theme print	½ yd.	2	7½" x 42"
Fabric A	⅝ yd.	5	3" x 42"
		1	3" x 14"
Fabric B	½ yd.	2	5¼" x 42"
		2	5¼" x 14"
Backing	1⅛ yds.		
Binding	⅜ yd.	4	2¼" x 42"
Batting	39" x 39"		

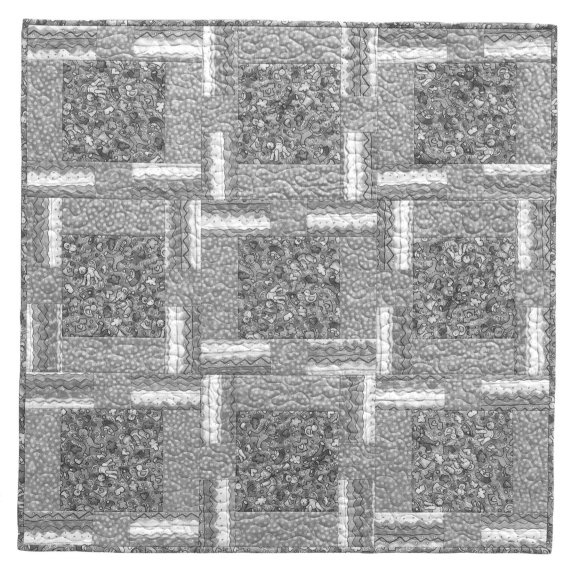

Sleepytime Tumble by Ursula Reikes, 1999, Ivins, Utah, 36½" x 36½".

Alternate quilt *Air Show* (see page 29)

DIRECTIONS

1. Make 2 of Strip Set #1. Cut 9 segments, each 7½" wide.

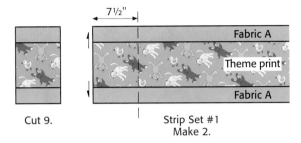

Cut 9.

Strip Set #1
Make 2.

2. Make 2 of Strip Set #2 in 2 different sizes. Cut 18 segments, each 3" wide.

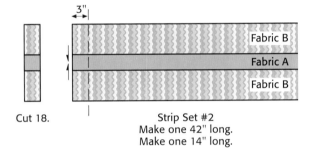

Cut 18.

Strip Set #2
Make one 42" long.
Make one 14" long.

3. Make 9 Barney's blocks.

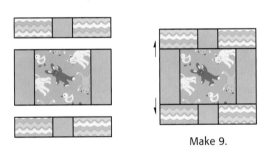

Make 9.

4. Arrange the blocks in 3 rows of 3 blocks each. Rotate the blocks as needed to form the design.

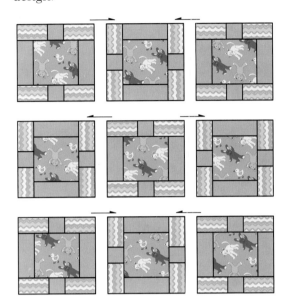

5. Join the blocks in horizontal rows. Join the rows.
6. Layer the quilt top with batting and backing; baste. Quilt as desired.
7. Bind the edges and add a label.

H BLOCK

For project directions and alternate quilt, see page 18.

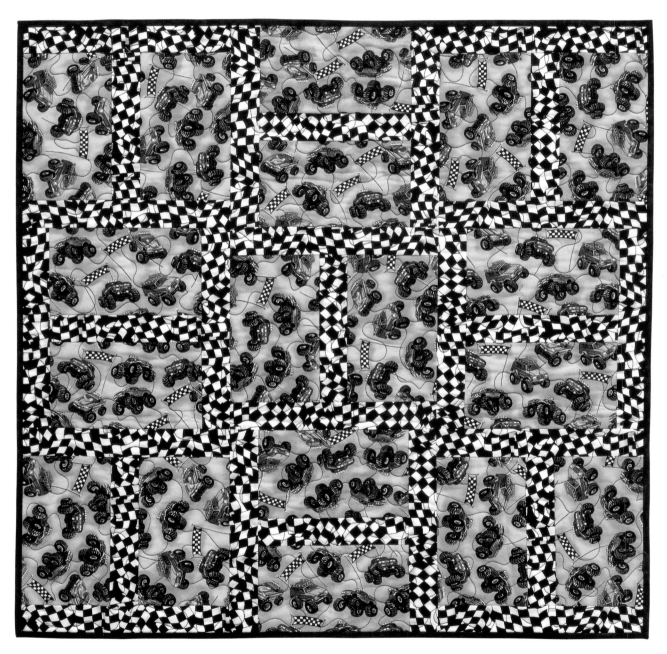

Road Rally by Ursula Reikes, 1999, Ivins, Utah, 33½" x 33½". Machine quilted by Janice Nelson.

BASKET WEAVE

For project directions and alternate quilt, see page 20.

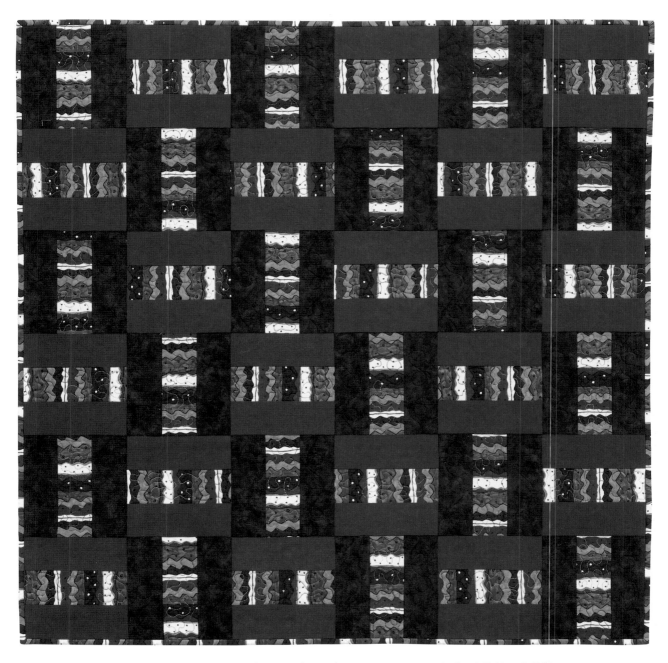

Bright Beginnings by Ursula Reikes, 1999, Ivins, Utah, 36½" x 36½".

SIMPLE PATCH

For project directions and alternate quilt, see page 22.

Wacky Wabbits by Ursula Reikes, 1999, Ivins, Utah, 27½" x 39½".

BARNEY'S BLOCK

For project directions and alternate quilt, see page 24.

Air Show by Ursula Reikes, 1999, Ivins, Utah, 36½" x 36½". Machine quilted by Janice Nelson.

NINE PATCH

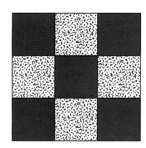

Nine Patch
Finished size: 6"

MATERIALS
42"-wide fabric

CUTTING
Cut all strips across the fabric width

Fabric	Yardage	FIRST CUT		SECOND CUT	
		# of Strips	Strip Size	# of Pieces	Piece Size
Theme print	½ yd.	2	6½" x 42"	12	6½" x 6½"
Fabric A	½ yd.	5	2½" x 42"		
Fabric B	⅜ yd.	4	2½" x 42"		
Inner border	⅜ yd.				
(sides)		2	2" x 30½"		
(top/bottom)		2	2" x 33½"		
Outer border	⅝ yd.	4	4½" x 33½"		
Corner squares	¼ yd.	1	4½" x 18"	4	4½" x 4½"
Backing	1½ yds.*				
Binding	⅜ yd.	5	2¼" x 42"		
Batting	44" x 44"				

*See page 12 for piecing the backing.

Doggy Days
by Ursula Reikes,
1999, Ivins, Utah,
41½" x 41½".

Alternate quilt
Pastel Patches
(see page 38)

DIRECTIONS

1. Make 2 of Strip Set #1. Make 1 of Strip Set #2. From Strip Set #1, cut 26 segments, each 2½" wide. From Strip Set #2, cut 13 segments, each 2½" wide.

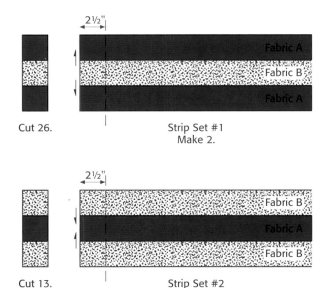

Cut 26.

Strip Set #1
Make 2.

Cut 13.

Strip Set #2
Make 1.

2. Make 13 Nine Patch blocks.

Make 13.

3. Arrange the blocks and squares in 5 rows.

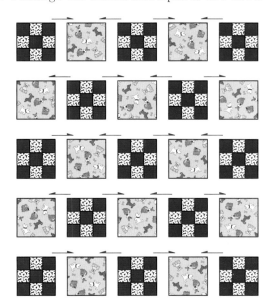

4. Join the blocks in horizontal rows. Join the rows.
5. Sew the inner border strips to the side edges of the quilt top first, then to the top and bottom edges. See "Borders with Straight-Cut Corners" on page 11.
6. Sew the outer border strips to the sides first. Add a corner square to each end of the remaining outer border strips and attach them to the top and bottom edges. See "Borders with Corner Squares" on page 12.

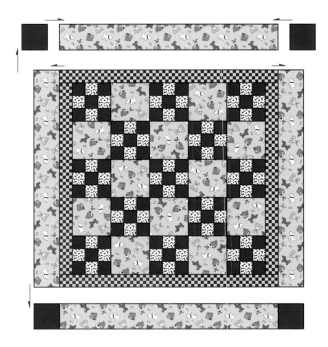

7. Layer the quilt top with batting and backing; baste. Quilt as desired.
8. Bind the edges and add a label.

TAM'S PATCH

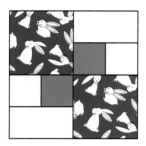

Tam's Patch
Finished size: 10"

		FIRST CUT		SECOND CUT	
Fabric	**Yardage**	**# of Strips**	**Strip Size**	**# of Pieces**	**Piece Size**
Theme print	⅜ yd.	2	5½" x 42"	12	5½" x 5½"
Fabric A	⅛ yd.	1	3" x 42"		
Fabric B	⅜ yd.	3	3" x 42"		
Inner border	¼ yd.				
(sides)		2	1½" x 30½"		
(top/bottom)		2	1½" x 22½"		
Outer border	⅔ yd.				
(sides)		2	5" x 32½"		
(top/bottom)		2	5" x 31½"		
Backing	1⅜ yd.				
Binding	⅜ yd.	4	2¼" x 42"		
Batting	34" x 44"				

MATERIALS
42"-wide fabric

CUTTING
Cut all strips across the fabric width

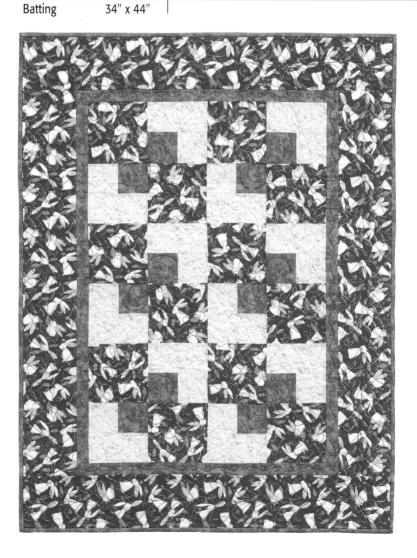

Funny Bunnies
by Ursula Reikes,
1999, Ivins, Utah,
31½" x 41½".
Machine quilted by
Janice Nelson.

Alternate quilt
Mouse Tales
(see page 39)

DIRECTIONS

1. Make 1 strip set. Cut 12 segments, each 3" wide.

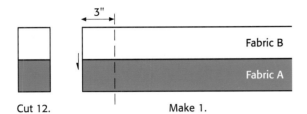

Cut 12.   Make 1.

2. Place the segments next to each other on top of a Fabric B strip, right sides together. Do not overlap the edges of the segments. Stitch. Cut between the segments, trimming away any excess fabric. Repeat with the remaining segments and Fabric B strip.

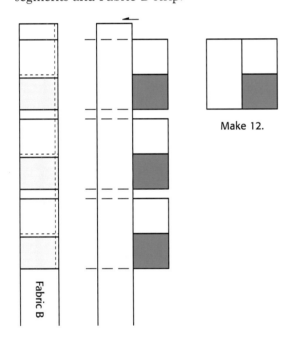

Make 12.

3. Make 6 Tam's Patch blocks.

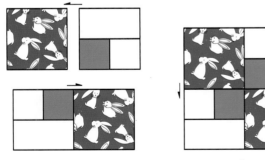

Make 6.

4. Arrange the blocks in 3 rows of 2 blocks each. Rotate the blocks so that the final seams butt together.

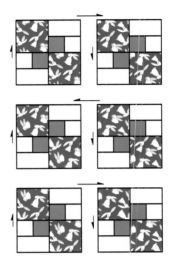

5. Join the blocks in horizontal rows. Join the rows.

6. Sew the inner border strips to the side edges of the quilt top first, then to the top and bottom edges. Repeat with the outer borders. See "Borders with Straight-Cut Corners" on page 11.

7. Layer the quilt top with batting and backing; baste. Quilt as desired.

8. Bind the edges and add a label.

TRIPLE RAILS

Triple Rail
Finished size: 6" x 8"

Nine Patch
Finished size: 6"

MATERIALS
42"-wide fabric

CUTTING
Cut all strips across the fabric width

| Fabric | Yardage | FIRST CUT | | SECOND CUT | |
		# of Strips	Strip Size	# of Pieces	Piece Size
Theme print	⅜ yd.*	1	8½" x 42"	4	8½" x 8½"
Fabric A	½ yd.	5	2½" x 42"		
		2	2½" x 6"		
Fabric B	⅝ yd.	7	2½" x 42"		
		1	2½" x 6"		
Backing	1⅛ yds.				
Binding	⅜ yd.	4	2¼" x 42"		
Batting	37" x 37"				

* You may need additional yardage if you want to center specific designs within each square.

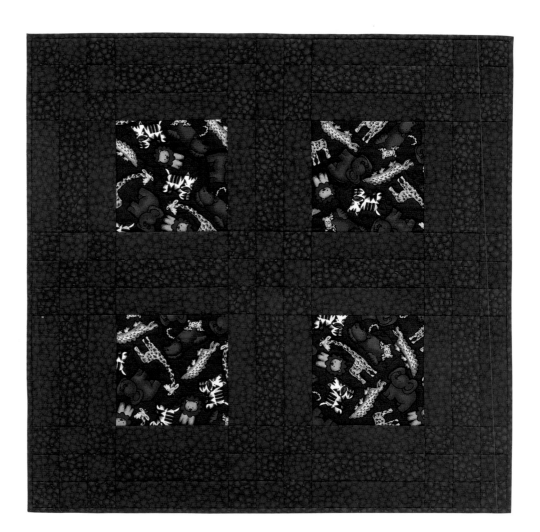

Comfy Critters
by Ursula Reikes,
1999, Ivins, Utah,
34½" x 34½".

Alternate quilt
Busy Bears
(see page 40)

DIRECTIONS

1. Make 2 of Strip Set #1 in 2 different lengths. Make 3 of Strip Set #2. From Strip Set #1, cut 18 segments, each 2½" wide. From Strip Set #2, cut 12 segments, each 8½" wide, and 9 segments, each 2½" wide.

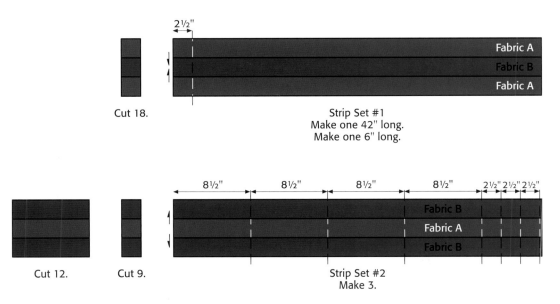

2½"

Fabric A
Fabric B
Fabric A

Cut 18.

Strip Set #1
Make one 42" long.
Make one 6" long.

8½" 8½" 8½" 8½" 2½" 2½" 2½"

Fabric B
Fabric A
Fabric B

Cut 12.   Cut 9.

Strip Set #2
Make 3.

2. Make 9 Nine Patch blocks.

Make 9.

3. Arrange the blocks, segments, and squares in rows.

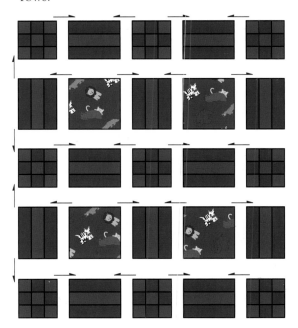

4. Join the units in horizontal rows. Join the rows.
5. Layer the quilt top with batting and backing; baste. Quilt as desired.
6. Bind the edges and add a label.

COURTHOUSE STEPS

Courthouse Steps
Finished size: 12"

MATERIALS 42"-wide fabric		CUTTING Cut all strips across the fabric width	
Fabric	**Yardage**	**# of Strips**	**Strip Size**
Theme print	½ yd.	1	6½" x 42"
		1	6½" x 21"
Fabric A	⅜ yd.	2	2" x 42"
		2	2" x 21"
Fabric B	⅜ yd.	5	2" x 42"
Fabric C	⅜ yd.	5	2" x 42"
Fabric D	½ yd.	6	2" x 42"
Backing	1¼ yd.		
Binding	½ yd.	4	2¼" x 42"
Batting	39" x 39"		

Dancing Dinos
by Ursula Reikes,
1999, Ivins, Utah,
36½" x 36½".

Alternate quilt
Toddler Trinkets
(see page 41)

DIRECTIONS

1. Make 2 strip sets in 2 different lengths. Cut 9 segments, each 6½" wide.

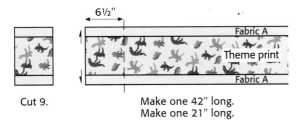

Cut 9.

Make one 42" long.
Make one 21" long.

2. Place the center segments next to each other on top of a Fabric B strip, right sides together. Do not overlap the edges of the segments. Stitch. Do not cut apart yet. You'll be able to sew 4 segments to each strip. Cut 1 of the Fabric B strips in half and sew the 9th unit to 1 half of the strip.

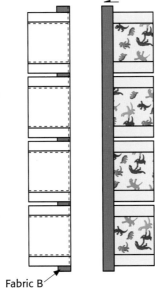

Fabric B

3. Turn the strip of sewn segments upside down and place the opposite side of the segments on top of another Fabric B strip, right sides together. Stitch. Sew the 9th unit to the other half of the Fabric B strip.

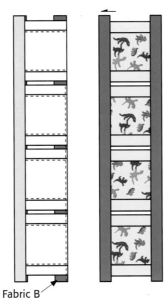

Fabric B

4. Lay the sewn units on the cutting mat. Use a ruler and rotary cutter to cut between the segments, trimming away any excess fabric.

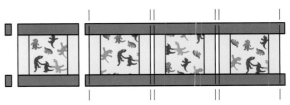

5. Repeat steps 2–4 using the sewn units and Fabric C strips.

6. Repeat steps 2–4 using the sewn units and Fabric D strips. You'll be able to sew only 3 segments to each strip.

7. Arrange the blocks in 3 rows of 3 blocks each. Rotate the blocks so the longest seams alternate from block to block.

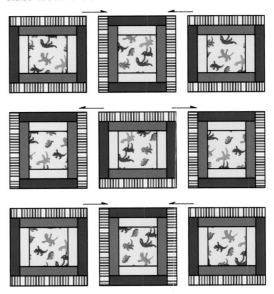

8. Join the blocks in horizontal rows. Join the rows.
9. Layer the quilt top with batting and backing; baste. Quilt as desired.
10. Bind the edges and add a label.

37

NINE PATCH

For project directions and alternate quilt, see page 30.

Pastel Patches by Ursula Reikes, 1999, Ivins, Utah, 41½" x 41½".

TAM'S PATCH

For project directions and alternate quilt, see page 32.

Mouse Tales by Ursula Reikes, 1999, Ivins, Utah, 31½" x 41½".

TRIPLE RAILS

For project directions and alternate quilt, see page 34.

Busy Bears by Ursula Reikes, 1999, Ivins, Utah, 34½" x 34½".

COURTHOUSE STEPS

For project directions and alternate quilt, see page 36.

Toddler Trinkets by Ursula Reikes, 1999, Ivins, Utah, 36½" x 36½".

ILLINOIS ROAD

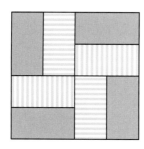

Illinois Road
Finished size: 6"

MATERIALS
42"-wide fabric

CUTTING
Cut all strips across the fabric width

Fabric	Yardage	FIRST CUT		SECOND CUT	
		# of Strips	Strip Size	# of Pieces	Piece Size
Theme print	½ yd.	2	6½" x 42"	12	6½" x 6½"
Fabric A	⅜ yd.	5	2" x 42"		
Fabric B	⅜ yd.	5	2" x 42"		
Inner border	⅛ yd.				
(sides)		2	1" x 30½"		
(top/bottom)		2	1" x 31½"		
Outer border	⅝ yd.				
(sides)		2	4½" x 31½"		
(top/bottom)		2	4½" x 39½"		
Backing	1½ yds.				
Binding	⅜ yd.	5	2¼" x 42"		
Batting	42" x 42"				

Taste of Honey
by Ursula Reikes,
1999, Ivins, Utah,
39½" x 39½".

Alternate quilt
Batter Up!
(see page 50)

DIRECTIONS

1. Make 5 strip sets. Cut 52 segments, each 3½" wide.

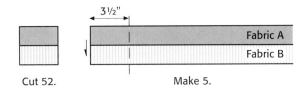

Cut 52.   Make 5.

2. Make 13 Illinois Road blocks.

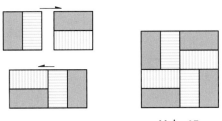

Make 13.

3. Arrange the blocks and squares in 5 rows of 5 blocks each.

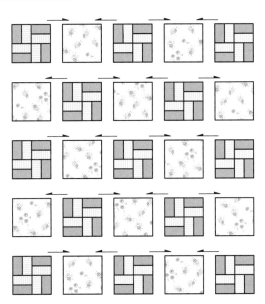

4. Join the blocks in horizontal rows. Join the rows.

5. Sew the inner border strips to the side edges of the quilt top first, then to the top and bottom edges. Repeat with outer border strips. See "Borders with Straight-Cut Corners" on page 11.

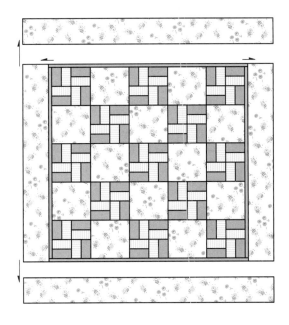

6. Layer the quilt top with batting and backing; baste. Quilt as desired.

7. Bind the edges and add a label.

FRIENDSHIP

Finished size: 6"

MATERIALS
42"-wide fabric

CUTTING
Cut all strips across the fabric width

Fabric	Yardage	FIRST CUT		SECOND CUT	
		# of Strips	Strip Size	# of Pieces	Piece Size
Theme print	1¼ yd.	3	6½" x 42"	16	6½" x 6½"
		3	5" x 42"	16	5" x 6½"
		1	5" x 20"	4	5" x 5"
Fabric A	⅜ yd.	3	3¾" x 42"	26	3¾" x 3¾"
Fabric B	¼ yd.	2	3" x 42"	26	3" x 3"
Backing	1⅛ yd.				
Binding	⅜ yd.	4	2¼" x 42"		
Batting	36" x 36"				

Buttercup Blues
by Ursula Reikes,
1999, Ivins, Utah,
33½" x 33½".

Alternate quilt
Soccer Skies
(see page 51)

DIRECTIONS

1. Draw a diagonal line from corner to corner on the wrong side of the 3¾" Fabric A squares and the 3" Fabric B squares.

2. Place a 3¾" Fabric A square on one corner of a 6½" Theme print square, right sides together. Stitch on the line. Trim, leaving a ¼"-wide seam allowance. Repeat with a 3" Fabric B square on the opposite diagonal corner.

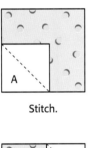 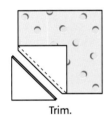 

Stitch.   Trim.   Press.

Stitch.   Trim.   Press.
Make 16.

3. Place a Fabric A square on the bottom right corner of 4 rectangles and on the bottom left corner of 4 rectangles. Stitch, trim, and press. Repeat with Fabric B squares on the remaining rectangles.

Make 4.   Make 4.

 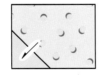

Make 4.   Make 4.

4. Place a Fabric A square on one corner of 2 of the 5" squares. Stitch, trim, and press. Place a Fabric B square on one corner of the remaining 5" squares. Stitch, trim, and press.

Make 2.   Make 2.

5. Arrange the units in rows, rotating them as needed to form the pattern.

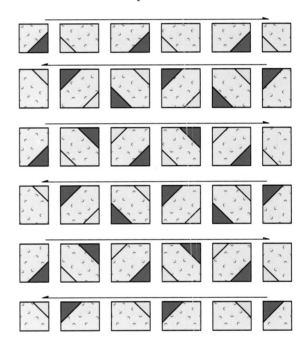

6. Join the units in horizontal rows. Join the rows.
7. Layer the quilt top with batting and backing; baste. Quilt as desired.
8. Bind the edges and add a label.

SICKLE

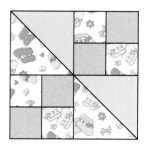

Sickle
Finished size: 12"

		FIRST CUT		SECOND CUT	
MATERIALS 42"-wide fabric				**CUTTING** Cut all strips across the fabric width	
Fabric	**Yardage**	**# of Strips**	**Strip Size**	**# of Pieces**	**Piece Size**
Theme print	⅞ yd.	2	6⅞" x 42"	9	6⅞" x 6⅞"
		3	3½" x 42"		
		1	3½" x 12"		
Fabric A	½ yd.	2	6⅞" x 42"	9	6⅞" x 6⅞"
Fabric B	½ yd.	3	3½" x 42"		
		1	3½" x 12"		
Backing	1⅛ yds.				
Binding	⅜ yd.	4	2¼" x 42"		
Batting	39" x 39"				

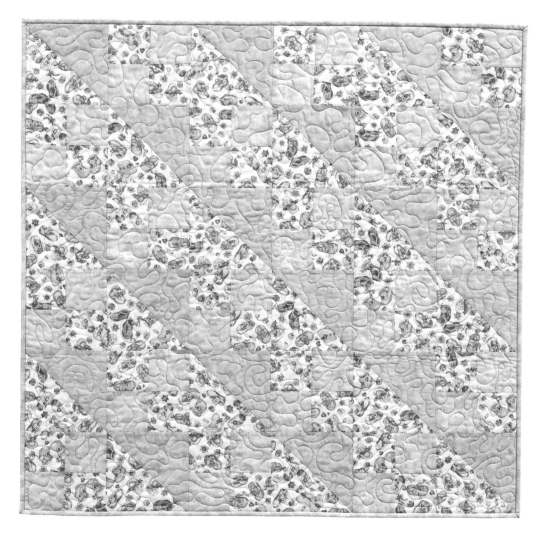

First Steps
by Ursula Reikes,
1999, Ivins, Utah,
36½" x 36½".

Alternate quilt
Marble Magic
(see page 52)

DIRECTIONS

1. Make 18 half-square triangle units as shown on page 8, using 6⅞" squares cut from the theme print and Fabric A.

Make 18.

2. Make 4 strip sets in 2 different sizes. Cut 36 segments, each 3½" wide.

Cut 36.

Make three 42" long.
Make one 12" long.

3. Join 2 segments to make a four-patch unit.

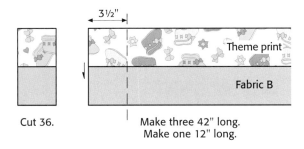

Make 18.

4. Make 9 Sickle blocks.

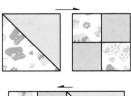

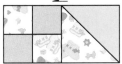

←— Press the final seam up in 6 of the blocks and down in the remaining 3 blocks.

Make 9.

5. Arrange the blocks in 3 rows of 3 blocks each. Rotate the blocks so that the final seams butt together.

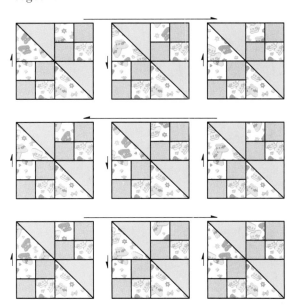

6. Join the blocks in horizontal rows. Join the rows.
7. Layer the quilt top with batting and backing; baste. Quilt as desired.
8. Bind the edges and add a label.

PINWHEEL

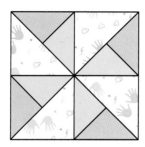

Pinwheel
Finished size: 12"

Cozy Pinwheels
by Ursula Reikes,
1999, Ivins, Utah,
35" x 47".
Machine quilted by
Janice Nelson.

Alternate quilt
Perky Pinwheels
(see page 53)

MATERIALS		FIRST CUT		SECOND CUT	
42"-wide fabric		Cut all strips across the fabric width			
Fabric	Yardage	# of Strips	Strip Size	# of Pieces	Piece Size
Theme print	½ yd.	2	6⅞" x 42"	12	6⅞" x 6⅞" ◺
Fabric A	½ yd.	2	7¼" x 42"	6	7¼" x 7¼" ⊠
Fabric B	½ yd.	2	7¼" x 42"	6	7¼" x 7¼" ⊠
Inner border	¼ yd.				
(sides)		2	1¾" x 36½"		
(top/bottom)		2	1¾" x 27"		
Outer border	⅝ yd.				
(sides)		2	4½" x 39"		
(top/bottom)		2	4½" x 27"		
Corner squares	¼ yd.	1	4½" x 18"	4	4½" x 4½"
Backing	1½ yds.				
Binding	⅜ yd.	5	2¼" x 42"		
Batting	38" x 50"				

DIRECTIONS

1. Join a Fabric A and a Fabric B triangle. Add a theme print triangle.

Make 24.

2. Make 6 Pinwheel blocks.

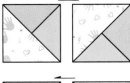
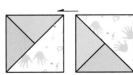
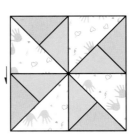

Make 6.

3. Arrange the blocks in 3 rows of 2 blocks each. Rotate the blocks so that the final seams butt together.

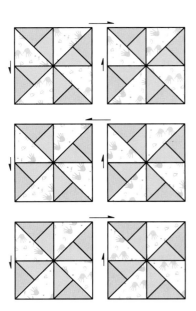

4. Join the blocks in horizontal rows. Join the rows.

5. Sew the inner border strips to the side edges of the quilt top first, then to the top and bottom edges. See "Borders with Straight-Cut Corners" on page 11.

6. Sew the outer border strips to the side edges first. Add a corner square to each end of the remaining outer border strips and attach them to the top and bottom edges. See "Borders with Corner Squares" on page 12.

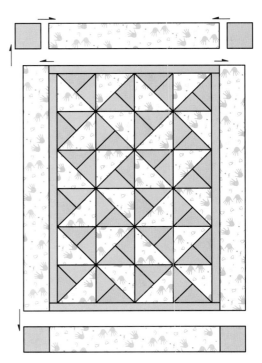

7. Layer the quilt top with batting and backing; baste. Quilt as desired.

8. Bind the edges and add a label.

ILLINOIS ROAD

For project directions and alternate quilt, see page 42.

Batter Up! by Ursula Reikes, 1999, Ivins, Utah, 39½" x 39½". Machine quilted by Janice Nelson.

FRIENDSHIP

For project directions and alternate quilt, see page 44.

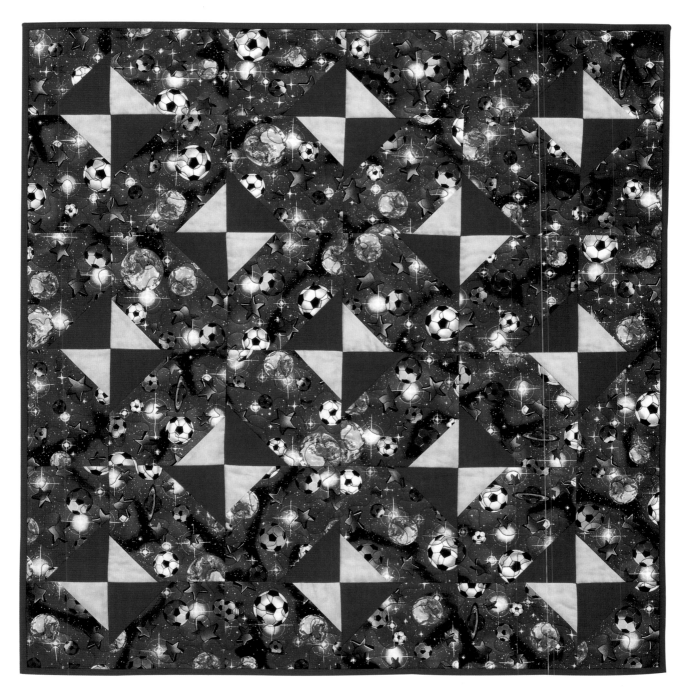

Soccer Skies by Ursula Reikes, 1999, Ivins, Utah, 33½" x 33½". Machine quilted by Janice Nelson.

SICKLE

For project directions and alternate quilt, see page 46.

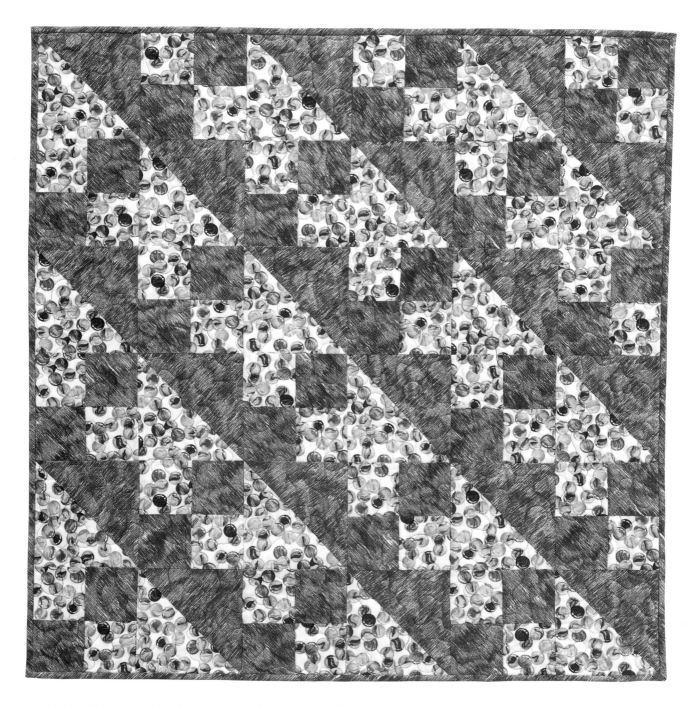

Marble Magic by Ursula Reikes, 1999, Ivins, Utah, 36½" x 36½". Machine quilted by Janice Nelson.

PINWHEEL

For project directions and alternate quilt, see page 48.

Perky Pinwheels by Ursula Reikes, 1999, Ivins, Utah, 35" x 47". Machine quilted by Janice Nelson.

CENTER STAR

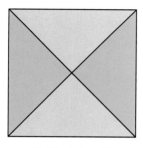

Finished size: 8"

MATERIALS
42"-wide fabric

CUTTING
Cut all strips across the fabric width

Fabric	Yardage	FIRST CUT		SECOND CUT	
		# of Strips	Strip Size	# of Pieces	Piece Size
Theme print	⅝ yd.	2	8½" x 42"	5	8½" x 8½"
Fabric A	⅔ yd.	1	9¼" x 42"	4	9¼" x 9¼" ⊠
		1	4½" x 42"	4	4½" x 8½"
		1	4½" x 18"	4	4½" x 4½"
Fabric B	½ yd.	1	9¼" x 42"	2	9¼" x 9¼" ⊠
		1	4⅞" x 42"	8	4⅞" x 4⅞" ◻
Backing	1⅛ yds.				
Binding	⅜ yd.	4	2¼" x 42"		
Batting	35" x 35"				

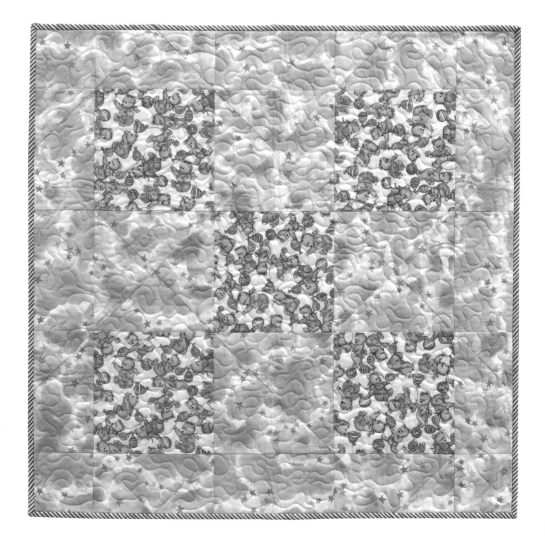

Sleepytime Teddies
by Ursula Reikes,
1999, Ivins, Utah,
32½" x 32½".

Alternate quilt
Blast Off!
(see page 62)

DIRECTIONS

1. Join 2 large Fabric A and 2 large Fabric B triangles.

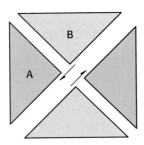

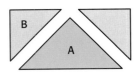

Make 4.

2. Join 2 small Fabric B triangles and a large Fabric A triangle.

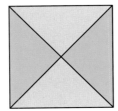

Make 8.

3. Arrange the units, squares, and rectangles in rows.

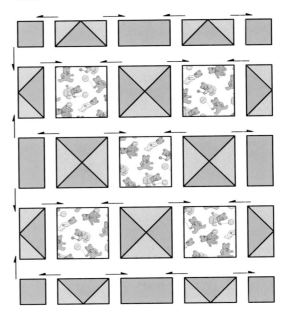

4. Join the units in horizontal rows. Join the rows.
5. Layer the quilt top with batting and backing; baste. Quilt as desired.
6. Bind the edges and add a label.

STRIPED SQUARES

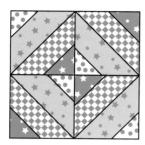

Striped Square A
Finished size: 11"

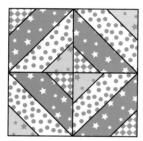

Striped Square B
Finished size: 11"

MATERIALS
42"-wide fabric

CUTTING
Cut all strips across the fabric width

Fabric	Yardage	# of Strips	Strip Size*
Fabric A	3/8 yd.	4	2¾" x 42"
Fabric B	3/8 yd.	4	2½" x 42"
Fabric C	3/8 yd.	3	2¾" x 42"
Fabric D	3/8 yd.	3	2½" x 42"
Inner & outer border	5/8 yd.	8	2½" x 42"
Middle border	¼ yd.	4	1½" x 42"
Backing	1½ yds.		
Binding	3/8 yd.	5	2¼" x 42"
Batting	35" x 46"		

* The fabric needs to be 42" wide after prewashing to cut the required number of squares. If your fabric is narrower than 42" wide, you will need to buy more fabric to cut additional strips for the strip set.

Note: You will need a 6" square ruler.

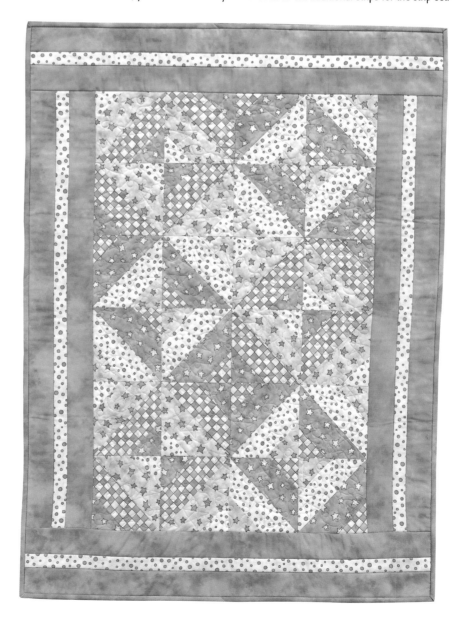

Heavenly Squares
by Ursula Reikes, 1999, Ivins, Utah, 32½" x 43½". Machine quilted by Janice Nelson.

Alternate quilt
Topsy Turvy
(see page 63)

DIRECTIONS

1. Make 1 large strip set, alternating Fabrics A, B, C, and D. Starting in the bottom right-hand corner, position the diagonal line of a 6"-square ruler on the 2nd seam line from the bottom. Cut around all 4 sides of the ruler. Continue cutting squares horizontally across the bottom. For the next 4 squares, position the diagonal line of the ruler on the 4th seam line from the bottom. Continue up the strip set to cut a total of 24 squares.

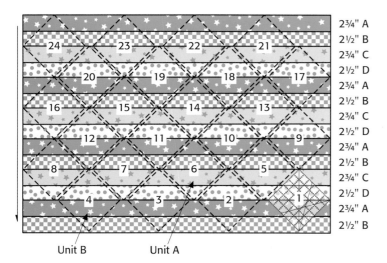

	2¾" A
	2½" B
	2¾" C
	2½" D
	2¾" A
	2½" B
	2¾" C
	2½" D
	2¾" A
	2½" B
	2¾" C
	2½" D
	2¾" A
	2½" B

Unit B   Unit A

Note: Be careful not to cut beyond the square ruler. Otherwise, you may cut into areas that will be needed for squares. Refer to the diagram often to make sure the diagonal line of the ruler is placed on the correct seam line before cutting each row of squares.

2. Join four A Units to make a Striped Square A. Rotate the squares so that the diagonal seam lines do not meet between the squares. This makes it easier to sew the squares together—no seams to match! Repeat with four B units to make a Striped Square B.

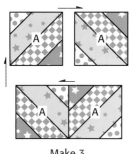   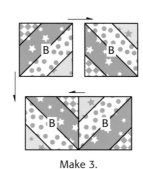

Make 3.   Make 3.

3. Arrange the blocks in 3 rows of 2 blocks each.

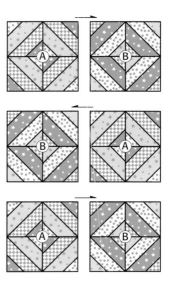

4. Join the blocks in horizontal rows. Join the rows.
5. Sew the inner, middle, and outer border strips together to make 4 pieced borders. Trim 2 of the border strips to 33½" and sew these to the side edges. Trim the remaining border strips to 32½" and sew these to the top and bottom edges. See "Borders with Straight-Cut Corners" on page 11.

6. Layer the quilt top with batting and backing; baste. Quilt as desired.
7. Bind the edges and add a label.

EASY VARIABLE STAR

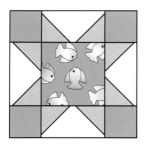

Easy Variable Star
Finished size: 12"

Go Fish!
by Ursula Reikes,
1999, Ivins, Utah,
35" x 47".

Alternate quilt
Spinning Stars
(see page 64)

MATERIALS
42"-wide fabric

CUTTING
Cut all strips across the fabric width

Fabric	Yardage	FIRST CUT		SECOND CUT	
		# of Strips	Strip Size	# of Pieces	Piece Size
Theme print	¼ yd.	1	6½" x 42"	6	6½" x 6½"
Fabric A	½ yd.	4	3¼" x 42"	48	3¼" x 3¼"
Fabric B	½ yd.	4	3½" x 42"	24	3½" x 6½"
Fabric C	⅜ yd.	2	3½" x 42"	24	3½" x 3½"
Inner border	¼ yd.				
(sides)		2	1¾" x 36½"		
(top/bottom)		2	1¾" x 27"		
Outer border	⅝ yd.				
(sides)		2	4½" x 39"		
(top/bottom)		2	4½" x 35"		
Backing	1½ yds.				
Binding	⅜ yd.	5	2¼" x 42"		
Batting	38" x 50"				

DIRECTIONS

1. Draw a diagonal from corner to corner on the wrong side of the 3¼" Fabric A squares.

2. Place a Fabric A square on one corner of a Fabric B rectangle, right sides together. Stitch on the line. Trim, leaving a ¼"-wide seam allowance. Repeat with another Fabric A square on the opposite corner.

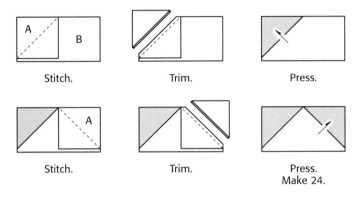

Stitch.   Trim.   Press.

Stitch.   Trim.   Press.
                                Make 24.

Note: By using smaller squares, you'll get perfect star points with no effort.

3. Make 6 Easy Variable Star blocks.

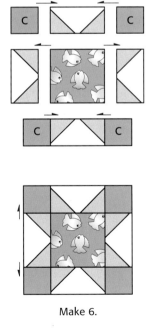

Make 6.

4. Arrange the blocks in 3 rows of 2 blocks each. Rotate the blocks so that the final seams butt together.

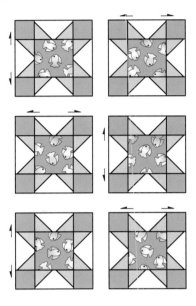

5. Join the blocks in horizontal rows. Join the rows.

6. Sew the inner border strips to the side edges of the quilt top first, then to the top and bottom edges. Repeat with outer border strips. See "Borders with Straight-Cut Corners" on page 11.

7. Layer the quilt top with batting and backing; baste. Quilt as desired.

8. Bind the edges and add a label.

FOUR-X STAR

Four-X Star
Finished size: 12½"

Pixies and Posies
by Ursula Reikes,
1999, Ivins, Utah,
38" x 38".

Alternate quilt
On the Move
(see page 65)

MATERIALS
42"-wide fabric

CUTTING
Cut all strips across the fabric width

Fabric	Yardage	FIRST CUT		SECOND CUT	
		# of Strips	Strip Size	# of Pieces	Piece Size
Theme print	⅜ yd.	1	8" x 42"	4	8" x 8"
Fabric A	¼ yd.	2	3⅜" x 42"	16	3⅜" x 3⅜"
Fabric B	¼ yd.	2	3⅜" x 42"	16	3⅜" x 3⅜"
Fabric C	⅜ yd.	3	3" x 42"	32	3" x 3"
Sashing/inner border	½ yd.				
(vertical sashing)		2	2" x 42"	2	2" x 13"
(horizontal sashing)				1	2" x 27"
(sides)		2	2" x 27"		
(top/bottom)		2	2" x 30"		
Outer border	⅝ yd.				
(sides)		2	4½" x 30"		
(top/bottom)		2	4½" x 38"		
Backing	1½ yds.				
Binding	⅜ yd.	4	2¼" x 42"		
Batting	41" x 41"				

DIRECTIONS

1. Make 32 half-square triangle units as shown on page 8, using 3⅜" squares cut from Fabrics A and B.

Make 32.

2. Make 4 Four-X Star blocks.

Make 4.

3. Arrange the blocks and sashing strips in rows.

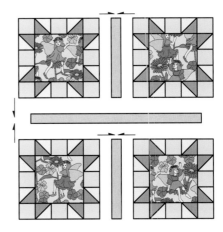

4. Join the blocks and sashing strip. Join the rows of blocks and horizontal sashing strip.

5. Sew the inner border strips to the side edges of the quilt top first, then to the top and bottom edges. Repeat with outer border strips. See "Borders with Straight-Cut Corners" on page 11.

6. Layer the quilt top with batting and backing; baste. Quilt as desired.

7. Bind the edges and add a label.

CENTER STAR

For project directions and alternate quilt, see page 54.

Blast Off! by Ursula Reikes, 1999, Ivins, Utah, 32½" x 32½". Machine quilted by Janice Nelson.

STRIPED SQUARES

For project directions and alternate quilt, see page 56.

Topsy Turvy by Ursula Reikes, 1999, Ivins, Utah, 32½" x 43½". Machine quilted by Janice Nelson.

EASY VARIABLE STAR

For project directions and alternate quilt, see page 58.

Spinning Stars by Ursula Reikes, 1999, Ivins, Utah, 35" x 47". Machine quilted by Janice Nelson.

FOUR-X STAR

For project directions and alternate quilt, see page 60.

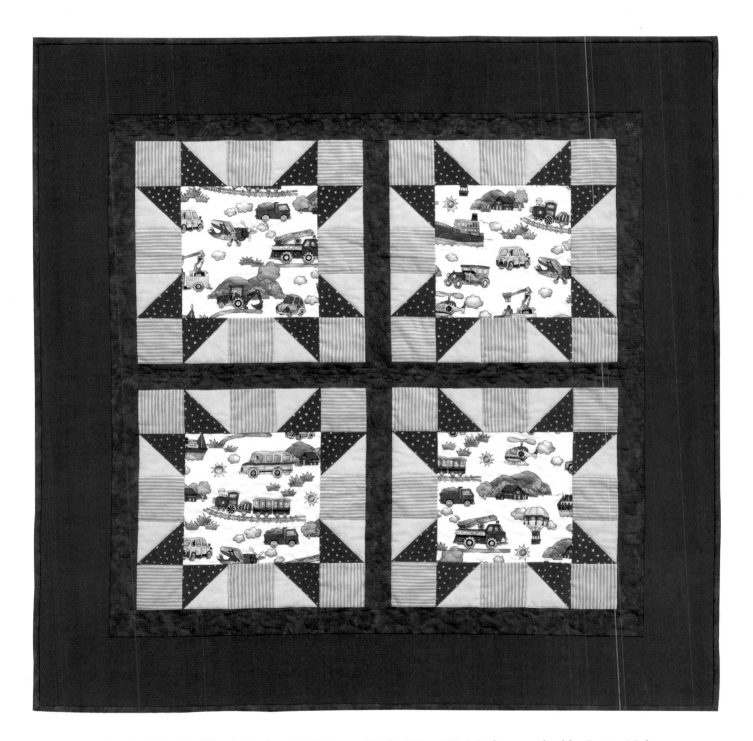

On the Move by Ursula Reikes, 1999, Ivins, Utah, 38" x 38". Machine quilted by Janice Nelson.

CHILDREN'S DELIGHT

Children's Delight
Finished size: 12"

MATERIALS
42"-wide fabric

CUTTING
Cut all strips across the fabric width

Fabric	Yardage	FIRST CUT		SECOND CUT	
		# of Strips	Strip Size	# of Pieces	Piece Size
Theme print	¼ yd.	1	6½" x 42"		
Fabric A	⅜ yd.	1	6½" x 42"		
		2	2½" x 42"		
Fabric B	¼ yd.	2	2½" x 42"		
Fabric C	⅜ yd.	4	2½" x 42"	12	2½" x 10½"
Fabric D	⅛ yd.	1	2½" x 15"	6	2½" x 2½"
Border	⅝ yd.				
(sides)		2	4½" x 36½"		
(top/bottom)		2	4½" x 32½"		
Backing	1½ yds.				
Binding	⅜ yd.	5	2¼" x 42"		
Batting	35" x 47"				

Hey Diddle Diddle
by Ursula Reikes,
1999, Ivins, Utah,
32½" x 44½".
Machine quilted by
Janice Nelson.

Alternate quilt
Giggling Gators
(see page 75)

DIRECTIONS

1. Make 1 each of Strip Sets #1 and #2. From Strip Set #1, cut 6 segments, each 6½" wide. From Strip Set #2, cut 12 segments, each 2½" wide.

Cut 6.

Strip Set #1
Make 1.

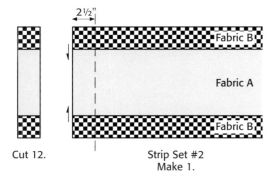

Cut 12.

Strip Set #2
Make 1.

2. Make 6 Children's Delight blocks.

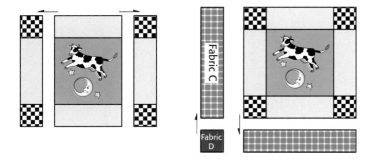

Press the final seam toward the center square on 3 blocks, and away from the center square on the remaining 3 blocks.

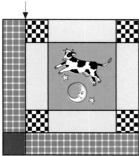

Make 6.

3. Arrange the blocks in 3 rows of 2 blocks each. Rotate the blocks so that the final seams butt together.

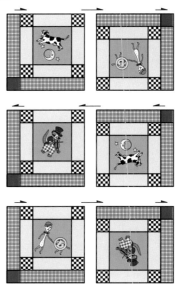

4. Join the blocks in horizontal rows. Join the rows.

5. Sew the border strips to the side edges of the quilt top first, then to the top and bottom edges. See "Borders with Straight-Cut Corners" on page 11.

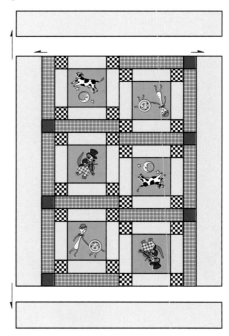

6. Layer the quilt top with batting and backing; baste. Quilt as desired.

7. Bind the edges and add a label.

BRAVE NEW WORLD

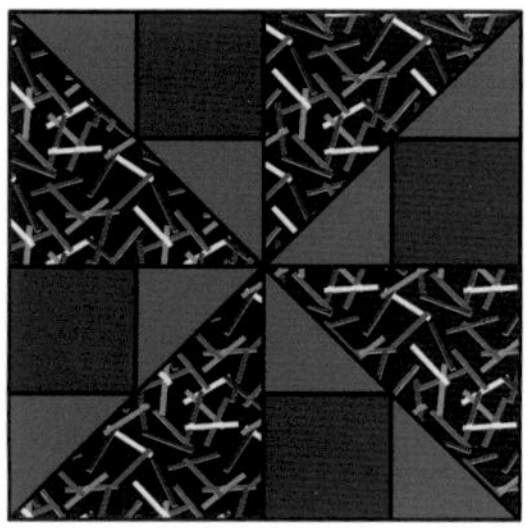

Brave New World
Finished size: 12"

MATERIALS 42"-wide fabric		CUTTING Cut all strips across the fabric width			
		FIRST CUT		SECOND CUT	
Fabric	Yardage	# of Strips	Strip Size	# of Pieces	Piece Size
Theme print	2/3 yd.	3	6 7/8" x 42"	12	6 7/8" x 6 7/8" ⍂
Fabric A	3/8 yd.	3	3 7/8" x 42"	24	3 7/8" x 3 7/8" ⍂
Fabric B	3/8 yd.	2	3 1/2" x 42"	24	3 1/2" x 3 1/2"
Inner border	1/4 yd.				
(sides)		2	1 3/4" x 36 1/2"		
(top/bottom)		2	1 3/4" x 27"		
Outer border	5/8 yd.				
(sides)		2	4 1/2" x 39"		
(top/bottom)		2	4 1/2" x 27"		
Corner squares	1/4 yd.	1	4 1/2" x 18"	4	4 1/2" x 4 1/2"
Backing	1 1/2 yds.				
Binding	3/8 yd.	4	2 1/4" x 42"		
Batting	38" x 50"				

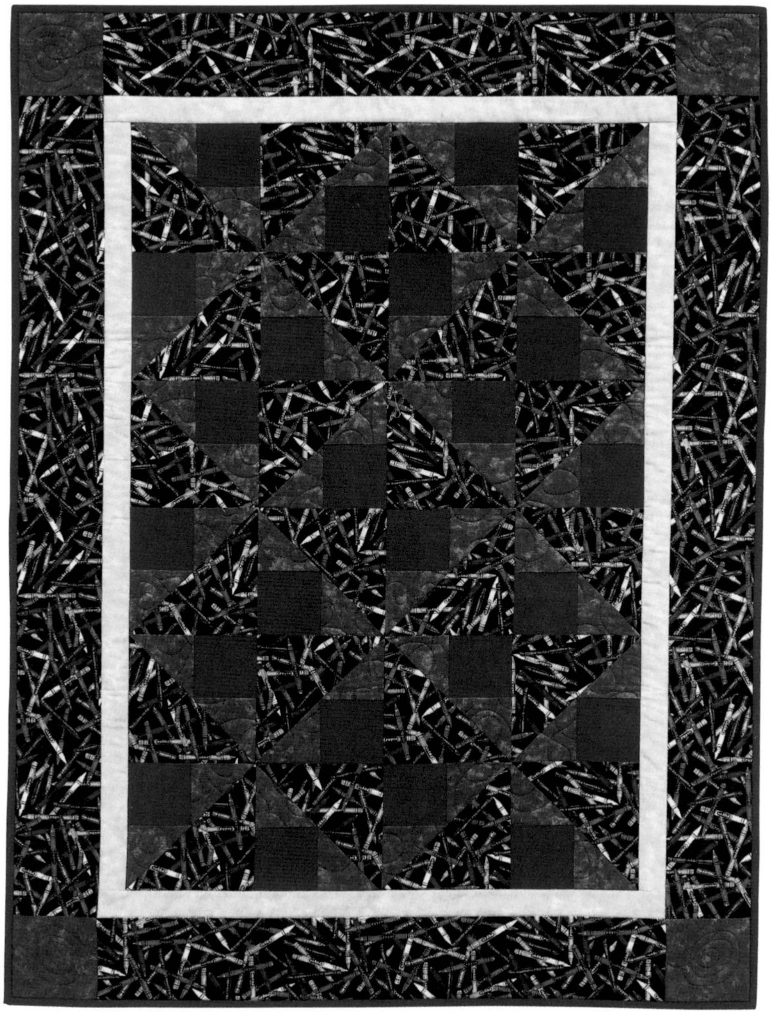

Color My World by Ursula Reikes, 1999, Ivins, Utah, 35" x 47".

Alternate quilt ***Night-night, Sleep Tight*** (see page 76)

DIRECTIONS

1. Join 2 Fabric A triangles and 1 Fabric B square. Add a theme print triangle.

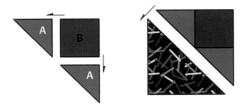

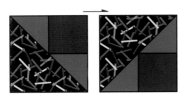

Make 24.

2. Make 6 Brave New World blocks.

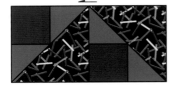

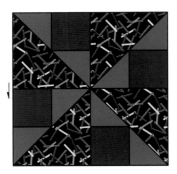

Make 6.

3. Arrange the blocks in 3 rows of 2 blocks each. Rotate the blocks so that the final seams butt together.

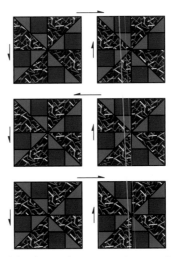

4. Join the blocks in horizontal rows. Join the rows.
5. Sew the inner border strips to the side edges of the quilt top first, then to the top and bottom edges. See "Borders with Straight-Cut Corners" on page 11.
6. Sew the outer border strips to the side edges first. Add a corner square to each end of the remaining outer border strips and attach them to the top and bottom edges. See "Borders with Corner Squares" on page 12.

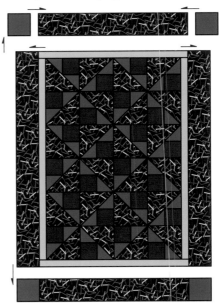

7. Layer the quilt top with batting and backing; baste. Quilt as desired.
8. Bind the edges and add a label.

LEFT AND RIGHT

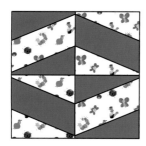

Left and Right
Finished size: 12"

Note: You will need a
6½" square ruler.

MATERIALS
42"-wide fabric

CUTTING
Cut all strips across the fabric width

| Fabric | Yardage | FIRST CUT | | SECOND CUT | |
		# of Strips	Strip Size	# of Pieces	Piece Size
Theme print	1 yd.	9	3¼" x 42"		
Fabric A	1 yd.	9	3¼" x 42"		
Inner border	¼ yd.				
(sides)		2	1½" x 36½"		
(top/bottom)		2	1½" x 26½"		
Outer border	⅝ yd.				
(sides)		2	4½" x 38½"		
(top/bottom)		2	4½" x 26½"		
Corner squares	¼ yd.	1	4½" x 18"	4	4½" x 4½"
Backing	1½ yds.				
Binding	⅜ yd.	5	2¼" x 42"		
Batting	37" x 49"				

Baby Bugs
by Ursula Reikes,
1999, Ivins, Utah,
34½" x 46½".

Alternate quilt
Baby Booties
(see page 77)

DIRECTIONS

1. Make 3 of Strip Set #1. Position a 6½" square ruler on the strip set, aligning the ½" mark on one side and the 6" mark on the opposite side with the seam lines. Cut around all 4 sides of the ruler. Be careful not to shift the ruler as you cut. Cut 12 squares from Strip Set #1.

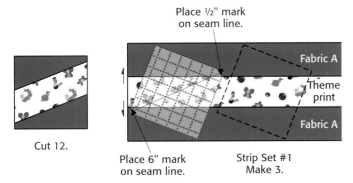

Place ½" mark on seam line.

Fabric A

Theme print

Fabric A

Cut 12.

Place 6" mark on seam line.

Strip Set #1
Make 3.

2. Make 3 of Strip Set #2. Refer to cutting directions in step 1 to cut the squares, except slant the ruler in the opposite direction. Cut 12 squares from Strip Set #2.

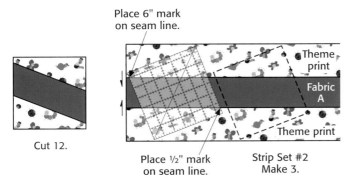

Place 6" mark on seam line.

Theme print

Fabric A

Theme print

Cut 12.

Place ½" mark on seam line.

Strip Set #2
Make 3.

3. Make 6 Left and Right blocks.

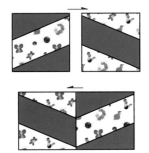 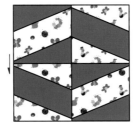

Make 6.

4. Arrange the blocks in 3 rows of 2 blocks each. Rotate the blocks so that the final seams butt together.

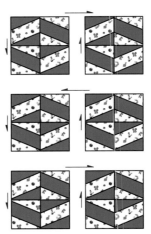

5. Join the blocks in horizontal rows. Join the rows.

6. Sew the inner border strips to the side edges of the quilt top first, then to the top and bottom edges. See "Borders with Straight-Cut Corners" on page 11.

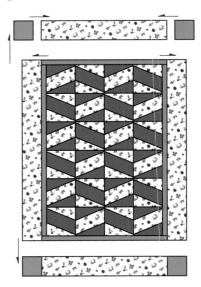

7. Sew the outer border strips to the side edges first. Add a corner square to each end of the remaining outer border strips and attach them to the top and bottom edges. See "Borders with Corner Squares" on page 12.

8. Layer the quilt top with batting and backing; baste. Quilt as desired.

9. Bind the edges and add a label.

DOUBLE ATTIC WINDOWS

Penguin Showers by Ursula Reikes, 1999, Ivins, Utah, 42½" x 42½".

Alternate quilt *Safari Windows* (see page 78)

MATERIALS
42"-wide fabric

CUTTING
Cut all strips across the fabric width

Double Attic Windows
Finished size: 10"

Fabric	Yardage	FIRST CUT		SECOND CUT	
		# of Strips	Strip Size	# of Pieces	Piece Size
Theme print	½ yd.	2	6½" x 42"	9	6½" x 6½"
Fabric A	½ yd.	1	2⅞" x 42"	9	2⅞" x 2⅞"
		2	2½" x 42"	8	2½" x 8½"
		2	2½" x 42"	1	2½" x 8½"
				9	2½" x 6½"
Fabric B	½ yd.	1	2⅞" x 42"	9	2⅞" x 2⅞"
		2	2½" x 42"	8	2½" x 8½"
		2	2½" x 42"	1	2½" x 8½"
				9	2½" x 6½"
Sashing/inner border ½ yd.					
(vertical sashing)		2	1½" x 42"	6	1½" x 10½"
(horizontal sashing)		2	1½" x 32½"		
(side borders)		2	1½" x 32½"		
(top/bottom borders)		2	1½" x 34½"		
Outer Border	⅝ yd.	4	4½" x 34½"		
Corner Squares	¼ yd.	1	4½" x 18"	4	4½" x 4½"
Backing	1½ yds.*				
Binding	⅜ yd.	5	2¼" x 42"		
Batting	45" x 45"				

* See page 12 for piecing the backing.

DIRECTIONS

1. Make 18 half-square triangle units as shown on page 8, using 2⅞" squares cut from Fabrics A and B.

Make 18.

2. Make 9 Double Attic Windows blocks.

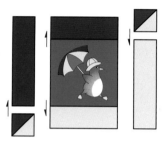

Make 9.

3. Arrange the blocks and sashing strips in rows.

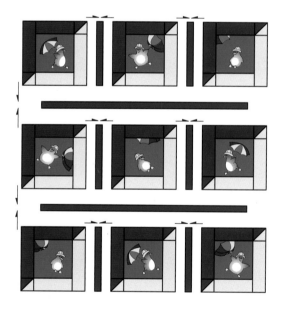

4. Join the blocks and sashing strips. Join the rows of blocks and horizontal sashing strips.

5. Sew the inner border strips to the side edges of the quilt top first, then to the top and bottom edges. See "Borders with Straight-Cut Corners" on page 11.

6. Sew the outer border strips to the side edges first. Add a corner square to each end of the remaining outer border strips and attach them to the top and bottom edges. See "Borders with Corner Squares" on page 12.

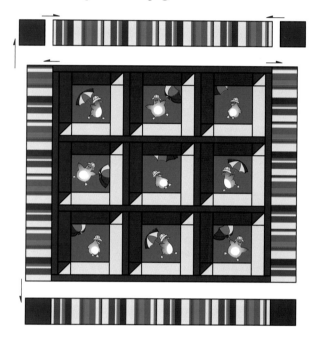

7. Layer the quilt top with batting and backing; baste. Quilt as desired.

8. Bind the edges and add a label.

CHILDREN'S DELIGHT

For project directions and alternate quilt, see page 66.

Giggling Gators by Ursula Reikes, 1999, Ivins, Utah, 32½" x 44½". Machine quilted by Janice Nelson.

BRAVE NEW WORLD

For project directions and alternate quilt, see page 68.

Night-night, Sleep Tight by Ursula Reikes, 1999, Ivins, Utah, 35" x 47".

LEFT AND RIGHT

For project directions and alternate quilt, see page 70.

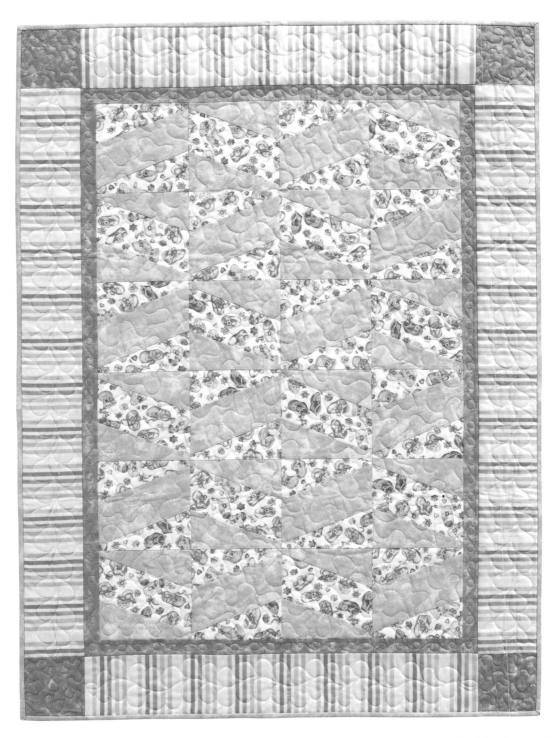

Baby Booties by Ursula Reikes, 1999, Ivins, Utah, 34½" x 46½". Machine quilted by Janice Nelson.

DOUBLE ATTIC WINDOWS

For project directions and alternate quilt, see page 72.

Safari Windows by Ursula Reikes, 1999, Ivins, Utah, 42½" x 42½".

ABOUT THE AUTHOR

Photo by John Reikes

Ursula Reikes continues to explore the possibilities for making quick and easy baby quilts. In this, her third book, Ursula has provided positive proof that baby quilts can be made in a variety of color combinations and in only a few hours. Like her first books, *Quilts for Baby: Easy as ABC*, and *More Quilts for Baby: Easy as ABC*, this book contains patterns designed for beginners but will appeal to quilters of all skill levels.

When Ursula isn't working as a technical editor for Martingale & Company, she's enjoying life with her husband, John, in the Red Rock canyons of southern Utah.

AUTHOR'S NOTE: Many people have asked what I intend to do with all the quilts I made for this book. Since most of my friends are beyond the baby stage, I really don't need forty baby quilts. In searching for a place where I could donate the quilts, I found a wonderful organization that makes quilts for foster babies and babies born alcohol or drug affected or infected with the HIV/AIDS virus. The group is called ABC Quilts (**A**t-risk **B**abies **C**rib Quilts). It is a worldwide, nonprofit volunteer organization. Since its inception in 1988, ABC has delivered over 325,000 quilts worldwide. I'm pleased that my quilts will be going to some very deserving babies. If you'd like to participate in the ABC Quilts project, please contact the organization at their main office:

ABC Quilts
569 First NH Turnpike, Suite #3
Northwood, NH 03261
(603) 942-9211
Email: info@abcquilts.mv.com
www.jbu.edu/abcquilts

Martingale & Company
Toll-free: 1-800-426-3126

International: 1-425-483-3313
24-Hour Fax: 1-425-486-7596

PO Box 118, Bothell, WA 98041-0118 USA

Web site: www.patchwork.com
E-mail: info@martingale-pub.com

Books from

That Patchwork Place®

Appliqué

Appliqué for Baby
Appliqué in Bloom
Baltimore Bouquets
Basic Quiltmaking Techniques for Hand Appliqué
Basic Quiltmaking Techniques for Machine Appliqué
Coxcomb Quilt
The Easy Art of Appliqué
Folk Art Animals
Fun with Sunbonnet Sue
Garden Appliqué
The Nursery Rhyme Quilt
Red and Green: An Appliqué Tradition
Rose Sampler Supreme
Stars in the Garden
Sunbonnet Sue All Through the Year

Beginning Quiltmaking

Basic Quiltmaking Techniques for Borders & Bindings
Basic Quiltmaking Techniques for Curved Piecing
Basic Quiltmaking Techniques for Divided Circles
Basic Quiltmaking Techniques for Eight-Pointed Stars
Basic Quiltmaking Techniques for Hand Appliqué
Basic Quiltmaking Techniques for Machine Appliqué
Basic Quiltmaking Techniques for Strip Piecing
The Quilter's Handbook
Your First Quilt Book (or it should be!)

Crafts

15 Beads
Fabric Mosaics
Folded Fabric Fun
Making Memories

Cross-Stitch & Embroidery

Hand-Stitched Samplers from I Done My Best
Kitties to Stitch and Quilt: 15 Redwork Designs
Miniature Baltimore Album Quilts
A Silk-Ribbon Album

Designing Quilts

Color: The Quilter's Guide
Design Essentials: The Quilter's Guide
Design Your Own Quilts
Designing Quilts: The Value of Value
The Nature of Design
QuiltSkills
Sensational Settings
Surprising Designs from Traditional Quilt Blocks
Whimsies & Whynots

Holiday

Christmas Ribbonry
Easy Seasonal Wall Quilts
Favorite Christmas Quilts from That Patchwork Place
Holiday Happenings
Quilted for Christmas
Quilted for Christmas, Book IV
Special-Occasion Table Runners
Welcome to the North Pole

Home Decorating

The Home Decorator's Stamping Book
Make Room for Quilts
Special-Occasion Table Runners
Stitch & Stencil
Welcome Home: Debbie Mumm
Welcome Home: Kaffe Fassett

Knitting

Simply Beautiful Sweaters
Two Sticks and a String

Paper Arts

The Art of Handmade Paper and Collage
Grow Your Own Paper
Stamp with Style

Paper Piecing

Classic Quilts with Precise Foundation Piecing
Easy Machine Paper Piecing
Easy Mix & Match Machine Paper Piecing
Easy Paper-Pieced Keepsake Quilts
Easy Paper-Pieced Miniatures
Easy Reversible Vests
Go Wild with Quilts
Go Wild with Quilts—Again!
It's Raining Cats & Dogs
Mariner's Medallion
Needles and Notions
Paper-Pieced Curves
Paper Piecing the Seasons
A Quilter's Ark
Sewing on the Line
Show Me How to Paper Piece

Quilting & Finishing Techniques

The Border Workbook
Borders by Design
A Fine Finish
Happy Endings
Interlacing Borders
Lap Quilting Lives!
Loving Stitches
Machine Quilting Made Easy
Quilt It!
Quilting Design Sourcebook
Quilting Makes the Quilt
The Ultimate Book of Quilt Labels

Ribbonry

Christmas Ribbonry
A Passion for Ribbonry
Wedding Ribbonry

Rotary Cutting & Speed Piecing

101 Fabulous Rotary-Cut Quilts
365 Quilt Blocks a Year Perpetual Calendar
All-Star Sampler
Around the Block with Judy Hopkins
Basic Quiltmaking Techniques for Strip Piecing
Beyond Log Cabin
Block by Block
Easy Stash Quilts
Fat Quarter Quilts
The Joy of Quilting
A New Twist on Triangles
A Perfect Match
Quilters on the Go
ScrapMania
Shortcuts
Simply Scrappy Quilts
Spectacular Scraps
Square Dance
Stripples Strikes Again!
Strips That Sizzle
Surprising Designs from Traditional Quilt Blocks

Traditional Quilts with Painless Borders
Time-Crunch Quilts
Two-Color Quilts

Small & Miniature Quilts

Bunnies by the Bay Meets Little Quilts
Celebrate! With Little Quilts
Easy Paper-Pieced Miniatures
Fun with Miniature Log Cabin Blocks
Little Quilts all Through the House
Living with Little Quilts
Miniature Baltimore Album Quilts
A Silk-Ribbon Album
Small Quilts Made Easy
Small Wonders

Surface Design

Complex Cloth
Creative Marbling on Fabric
Dyes & Paints
Fantasy Fabrics
Hand-Dyed Fabric Made Easy
Jazz It Up
Machine Quilting with Decorative Threads
New Directions in Chenille
Thread Magic
Threadplay with Libby Lehman

Topics in Quiltmaking

Bargello Quilts
The Cat's Meow
Even More Quilts for Baby
Everyday Angels in Extraordinary Quilts
Fabric Collage Quilts
Fast-and-Fun Stenciled Quilts
Folk Art Quilts
It's Raining Cats & Dogs
Kitties to Stitch and Quilt: 15 Redwork Designs
Life in the Country with Country Threads
Machine-Stitched Cathedral Windows
More Quilts for Baby
A New Slant on Bargello Quilts
Patchwork Pantry
Pink Ribbon Quilts
Quilted Landscapes
The Quilted Nursery
Quilting Your Memories
Quilts for Baby
Quilts from Aunt Amy
Whimsies & Whynots

Watercolor Quilts

More Strip-Pieced Watercolor Magic
Quick Watercolor Quilts
Strip-Pieced Watercolor Magic
Watercolor Impressions
Watercolor Quilts

Wearables

Easy Reversible Vests
Just Like Mommy
New Directions in Chenille
Quick-Sew Fleece
Variations in Chenille